Asset Protection
&Retirement
in Massachusetts:

Avoiding Financial Disaster Caused By A Nursing Home Stay

Protecting the Family Home, Savings, and Retirement Accounts from Nursing Home Costs

Avoiding Senior Citizen Tax Traps and the Federal and State Estate Tax

Edward D. Beasley, JD, LLM
David H. Ferber, JD
Gregory B. Gagne, ChFC

Library of Congress Control No: 2006908257
ISBN 978-0-9789845-0-2   (0-9789845-0-1)

Printed in the United States of America by Mennonite Press, Inc., Newton, Kansas.

Book Design by Kathy D. Danewitz

Published by Beasley & Ferber, PA, Concord New Hampshire, and Affinity Investment Group, LLC, Exeter, New Hampshire.

For additional copies, send $24.95 plus $3.00 shipping and handling per book to:

Beasley & Ferber, PA	or	Affinity Investment Group, LLC
55 Hall Street		12 String Bridge
Concord, NH 03301		Exeter, NH 03833
(603) 225-5010		(603) 778-6436

Dedication

This book is dedicated to our clients, senior citizens, who have made it through a lifetime of sacrifices including wars and the depression, only wishing to protect the modest nest egg they have created for the ones they love.

Edward D. Beasley
David H. Ferber

This book is dedicated to my wife Diana, and my three children Lucas, Emily and Sarah who are a constant reminder of life's blessings.

Gregory B. Gagne

Table of Contents

About the Authors

Edward D. Beasley, JD, LL.M.: Attorney Beasley is the founder of Beasley & Ferber, P.A. an Estate Planning and Elder Law Firm with offices in Concord, Bedford, Nashua and Portsmouth, New Hampshire and North Andover, Massachusetts. He received his Bachelor's Degree, Summa Cum Laude, Phi Beta Kappa, from Dartmouth College (1974), his Juris Doctor Degree, Cum Laude, from Washington & Lee University (1978) and his LL.M. Degree in Taxation from Boston University (1982).

Mr. Beasley has written and published numerous articles on Estate Planning and Elder law including "Trusts For the Average Person," "The Nursing Home Crunch," and "The Ethics of Medicaid Planning." He has appeared as a featured guest on NBC's National Nightly News with Tom Brokaw in a segment entitled "Inheritance Disputes." Attorney Beasley was also featured in a USA TODAY cover story entitled: "Fighting Over the Care of Aging Parents." He is co-author of the book, "Alzheimer's Disease: Fighting for Financial Survival, "The Nursing Home Crunch" and Asset Protection and Retirement in New Hampshire. He lectures frequently on the topic of Elder Law and the legal steps available to protect the life savings of a loved one afflicted with Alzheimer's Disease. He has been a guest on New Hampshire Public Radio, speaking about nursing home planning.

Mr. Beasley is former Chair of the Elder Law Committee of the American Bar Association (General Practice, Solo and Small Firm Section). He is also a member of the National Academy of Elder Law Attorneys. Mr. Beasley is recognized nationally as an expert in the field of Elder Law, Medicaid and Nursing Home Planning, and Asset Preservation techniques for those afflicted with dementia in general and the dementing illnesses known as Alzheimer's Disease, Huntington's Disease and Amyothrophic Lateral Sclerosis (Lou Gehrig's Disease), in particular.

David H. Ferber, JD: Attorney Ferber is a partner with Beasley & Ferber, P.A. He received his Bachelor's Degree in Psychology, Magna Cum Laude, Phi Beta Kappa, from Columbia University (1981) and his Juris Doctor Degree from Columbia University Law School (1984), where he was a member of the Columbia Human Rights Law Review.

Mr. Ferber is a nationally-published author of articles on Estate and Medicaid Planning, including articles on Charitable Remainder Trusts, The Use of Annuities in Medicaid Planning, The Use of Disclaimers in Estate Planning, Qualified Personal Residence Trusts and the Joint Revocable Trust as a Tool for Estate and Medicaid Planning, among others. He is also the author of articles on Estate Planning for the Concord Monitor, Concord, N.H., and the Laconia Citizen, Laconia, N.H. He is co-author of the book, "Alzheimer's Disease: Fighting for Financial Survival," "The Nursing Home Crunch" and Asset Protection and

Retirement in New Hampshire. He is a frequent lecturer on Estate and Medicaid Planning, having given presentations on Estate Planning for the State of New Hampshire Division of Elderly and Adult Services, for other attorneys, social workers and for the general public. He has been a guest on WMUR-TV, speaking about nursing home planning.

Mr. Ferber is former Vice Chair and Newsletter Editor of Elder Law Committee of the American Bar Association (General Practice, Solo and Small Firm Section), and is a member of the National Academy of Elder Law Attorneys. He is on the board of directors of the New Hampshire Family Support Partnerships, and is a former board member of the New Hampshire Coalition Against Elder Abuse, a former Commissioner of the Laconia, New Hampshire, Conservation Commission and a former board member of the Stamford, Connecticut, Shelter for the Homeless. He is a member of the bars of New Hampshire, Massachusetts, Maine and Connecticut.

Gregory B. Gagne, ChFC: Mr. Gagne is the founder of Affinity Investment Group, LLC, an investment advisory firm registered with the United States Securities and Exchange Commission. His firm offers wealth management and distribution planning services for retirees or those planning to retire.

After earning his Bachelor of Science, a dual degree in economics and finance, from Bentley College in 1992, Greg became a Chartered Financial Consultant in 2001 following completion of courses in estate planning, financial planning, business planning, income tax, and retirement and pension planning through the American College.

A member of the New Hampshire Chapter of the Society of Financial Service Professionals, Greg is also past president of the New Hampshire Association of Insurance and Financial Advisors, having served previously in many chairs of its local board. He now serves on a national committee for the organization. He is a member of the Financial Planning Association.

Greg has garnered national exposure in professional trade magazine articles and is co-author of the book Asset Protection and Retirement in New Hampshire. He frequently is featured writing on topics such as practice management, planning techniques and goal setting. He is a sought-after speaker on these subjects.

Foreward

"Many of life's failures are by people who did not realize how close they were to success when they gave up."
                                                    Thomas A Edison

Our forefathers had the foresight to envision the wonderful opportunities our country could provide for the average person. Their foundation laid a path for hard-working Americans to follow and then eventually create new paths of prosperity in our land.

Hard-working men and women spent their lives in the nearby mill buildings in the Merrimack Valley creating their own version of the "American Dream." The problem then and today is that so many folks were focused on their work that they never took the time to properly create a plan for their financial affairs.

This book will teach you about the issues retirees face and the various techniques used to protect the nest egg that you have spent a lifetime creating.

This book is intended to be an easily understood guide for the average person. You need not be a legal or an investment expert to understand the concepts and "blueprints" of the time-tested and proven methods to creating a lasting financial plan for you and your family.

Most retirees grew up in an era of frugality and saving. The valuable lessons of resourcefulness have been ingrained into many seniors' psyches. Many seniors have done without, saved considerable sums of money, and built a substantial net worth. It is time to take the next step and protect what you have created.

Chapter 1:
What is Your American Dream?

"If parents pass enthusiasm along to their children, they will leave them an estate of incalculable value."

Thomas A Edison

This question is not easily answered. There are many correct answers, including, health, happiness, and significant financial assets. When all the various answers are boiled down they equate to time freedom and financial freedom; the ability to do what you want when you want and how you want.

We have enjoyed the opportunity to interview hundreds and hundreds of families in the Northeast while preparing this book to ask this very question; what is your American Dream? We have learned a great deal over the last several years from the answer to this question and are honored to share the results with you.

For most folks it is the ability to afford the "wants "and not just the "needs "of life and the capacity to enjoy sharing with their families and community. Most families are concerned with protecting their nest egg, creating a lasting legacy for their family and helping others less fortunate along the way. Yes, we want to increase our net worth, but what about achieving and maintaining a balance during the "golden" years?

The issues of the utmost importance to the people my firm has interviewed over the past several years include:

- Health
- Happiness
- Preservation of capital
- Protection of assets in the event of a nursing home stay
- Assisting the grandchildren in obtaining higher education
- Philanthropic intentions
- Instilling values into the younger generations
- Taking the "trip of a lifetime"
- Protecting their spouse
- Leaving a legacy for children

It takes a sound business plan for your finances to achieve these various goals. We will spend the remainder of this book reviewing the building blocks you should utilize to fulfill your goals and objectives and to create a legacy for you and your family. Learn the valuable lessons from others mistakes so that you will not have to repeat them. Take the time to get your financial affairs in good order to guard you against life's uncertainties.

Chapter 2:
Basic Estate Planning –
Wills, Trusts, and Powers of
Attorney in Massachusetts

A. Wills

Every adult, regardless of age and level of assets, should have a solid estate plan. Preparing an estate plan will ensure that your assets will pass to the people you want in the manner you want, and will also protect you and your family in the event you become incapacitated or disabled. An estate plan can be designed to minimize taxes, probate fees and administration costs, and most important, to give you piece of mind about your family's security. Four documents typically go into a Massachusetts estate plan: trust, will, durable power of attorney and health care proxy.

A will, of course, is a legal document that provides for the passage of assets to the heirs on death. [1] A surprising number of people think that a will avoids probate. However, exactly

---

1   Technically, an "heir" is someone who will inherit your estate through the laws of intestate succession if you do not have a will. In this book, when we use the word "heirs," we will use it in the non-technical sense, as being synonymous with "beneficiaries."

the opposite is true: A will is your family's admission ticket to probate court. When someone dies in Massachusetts, the will is filed with the probate court for the county in which he or she lived, along with a petition for appointment of an executor. (Most people think that the person you name in the will as executor automatically becomes executor on your death. This is not the case. Rather, the probate judge has to formally appoint the executor before he can act.

Even though a document might have the word "Will" in the title, it does not automatically qualify to be a valid will. If you type your wishes on your computer, or if you hand write your wishes on the proverbial cocktail napkin, you have not created a valid will, because, to be valid, a will must be prepared strictly in accordance with certain formalities required by law. First and foremost, the will needs to have been signed by the decedent in the presence of two witnesses. All three persons (testator and witnesses) need to have signed in the presence of each other and in the presence of a notary public. Any adult who is mentally competent can be a witness. However, if one of the witnesses to a will is also a beneficiary of that will, then the gift to that person is void unless two other disinterested witnesses sign the will. (To be safe, the witnesses should be completely independent. They should not be family members or beneficiaries under the will.) The notary needs to sign a formal affidavit attesting to the manner of execution. If such an affidavit, known as a "self-proving affidavit," has not been signed, then one of the witnesses will need to testify in court as to the manner of execution of the will.

As long as you are mentally competent and not under duress, you can always revoke a will you have previously made. Under Massachusetts General Laws, Chapter 191, Sec. 8, a will may be revoked in rather dramatic fashion by "burning, tearing, canceling or obliterating it with the intention of revoking it," or, with less fanfare, simply by making another will. If you prepare a will and then get divorced, any provision in the will benefiting your ex-spouse is automatically revoked. Most wills state that the executor is to serve without bond, or with a minimum bond. The court will typically honor this direction if the parties who are interested to the will agree. After the will has been accepted by the court and the bond has been purchased (if required), then the court formally appoints the executor by issuing a" Certificate of Appointment." This is an official document with the court seal.

Within three months after the executor has been appointed, he must mail the beneficiaries a notice that bequests have been made to them. The executor then files with the probate court an affidavit showing the names of those notified and the addresses to which notices were mailed. Also within three months of appointment, the executor makes an inventory of all of the assets to be probated, and reports that inventory, under oath, to the court. The inventory stays on file with the court and is a matter of public record. Next, the executor collects the assets and pays the decedent's final expenses, debts and taxes. If creditors have any claims against the estate, those claims are presented to the executor. If the claim is valid, then the executor must pay it out of the decedent's assets. If the executor believes that the claim is not valid, then he notifies the creditor that the claim is being denied. It is then up to the creditor to decide whether to bring suit to enforce the claim. Of course, if the executor and creditor agree, the claim may be compromised, or settled. If there are any estate taxes due either the Commonwealth or the IRS, the executor, before closing the estate, needs to obtain a release from the relevant taxing authority, *i.e.,* a document stating that all taxes are paid. At the end of the probate proceedings, before the assets can be distributed to the beneficiaries, the executor makes a report to the judge of all that he has done, as well as a report of the income and expenditures of the estate. This report is known as an "accounting." It is only after the judge approves of the accounting that the assets can be distributed to the heirs.

If the assets to be probated do not exceed $15,000 plus a car, then full-fledged probate is not required. Rather, a simplified procedure known as "Voluntary Administration" is used. Under Voluntary Administration, there are many fewer formalities and requirements than under regular probate administration.

B. Trusts

Someone who wants to avoid probate for his family can prepare a revocable trust, also known as a living trust. In large part, the trust says the same thing as a will, *i.e.,* who is going to inherit the assets, and who the trustee (the functional equivalent of an executor) is to be. The crucial difference between a trust and a will, however, is that the will is subject to probate upon death, whereas the trust is not.

A trust has three parties, the "grantor," who is the person who sets up the trust, the "trustee," who is the person who manages the trust, and the "beneficiaries," who are the persons or organizations (such as charities) that will benefit from the trust. [2] When you set up a living trust,

---

2   Recent laws in some states allow animals to be trust beneficiaries.

you wear all three hats, in that you are the grantor, trustee and beneficiary. You place your assets in the name of the trust, and then go about your business exactly as usual. When you die, or if you become incompetent, a successor trustee of your choice, usually one or two of your children, takes over management of the trust. Ultimately, at your death, the beneficiaries you have named in the trust inherit the trust assets without probate. In almost all cases, there are no legal fees to settle the trust, and settlement of your estate proceeds quickly and privately. The formalities and procedures described in the preceding section concerning probate do not occur. Years ago, mainly the wealthy did trusts, while most other people did wills. These days, living trusts have become standard estate planning tools for people of moderate means, not only just the wealthy.

Whether you opt for a will or a living trust in your estate plan, special care must be taken if your spouse is ill or might need nursing home care. Most wills and trusts for married people naturally leave the assets to the surviving spouse. If one of the spouses is or might become a permanent resident of a nursing home, however, care must be taken to avoid automatically naming that spouse as beneficiary. Let's say that one spouse is in the nursing home and is receiving Medicaid benefits. The couple has a set of wills or trust that leaves everything to the surviving spouse. If the healthy spouse unexpectedly dies first, then all of the assets will go to the nursing home spouse. He or she will immediately lose Medicaid coverage, and will have to spend down the inheritance. It is likely that the children will receive nothing. To avoid this situation, the couple could have written their estate planning documents to say that if the healthy spouse dies first, the assets would pass to the children instead of the ill spouse. They should also give thought to amending the beneficiary designations on their life insurance and IRAs in the same way.

A trust is usually accompanied by a special type of will known as a "Pourover Will." A pourover will is meant to capture any miscellaneous or "orphan" assets that are not part of the trust. To understand this, you need to know that there are actually four ways of passing assets at death. We have already looked at two of them: wills and trusts. The other two are joint tenancies and beneficiary arrangements. We are all familiar with joint tenancies. Many bank accounts and other financial or real estate assets are held in titles such as, "John and Linda, JTWROS." This abbreviation stands for "joint tenants with rights of survivorship." The people whose names are on the account are known, not surprisingly, as "joint tenants." The essence of a joint tenancy is that, on the death of a joint tenant, the other joint tenant takes over ownership of the asset automatically. [3] The final way of passing assets at death, that of naming a beneficiary, is also familiar. Life insurance, annuities and IRAs/401ks all have, or rather, are supposed to have, named beneficiaries.

A pourover will is meant to apply to any asset that is not subject to any of the above four arrangements. Take the example of Emily. Emily owns a house, savings account, checking account, IRA, US savings bonds and a car. Her house and savings account are in the name of her living trust. The checking account is subject to a joint tenancy with Emily and her son. Her IRA names her daughter as

---

3   Do not confuse joint tenancy with "tenancy in common," as they are exact opposites, and never, ever say "joint tenants in common," in a legal document as it is a meaningless phrase.

beneficiary. The savings bonds and car are in Emily's sole name. When Emily dies, the house and savings automatically go the trust beneficiaries. The checking account goes to her son. The IRA goes to her daughter. The savings bonds and car pass through the pourover will. The beneficiary of the pourover will is Emily's trust. Therefore, the trust will receive the savings account and car, and, in turn, will pass those assets to the trust beneficiaries. Therefore, as you can see, the pourover will makes sure that any asset that Emily overlooked will be properly administered at her death. The only drawback, however, is that assets passing through the pourover will are subject to probate. In order to avoid this result, anyone who has prepared a trust and pourover will should take a careful look at his assets, in order to make sure that on death, none of those assets need to be probated. A truly successful estate plan containing a trust will avoid all probate, and care should be taken to properly title all assets to make sure this result is obtained.

C. Durable Financial Powers of Attorney

Someone who has become mentally (and sometimes physically) incompetent does not have the legal capacity to transact business. For example, such a person cannot pay bills, sign tax returns, buy or sell property or make contracts. When an incompetent person has not done adequate estate planning, someone such as a spouse, adult child or other interested party must petition the probate court to become "Guardian over the Estate." The court-appointed guardian can then transact business as representative for the incompetent person. There are a number of statutory reasons that the Probate Courts in Massachusetts will grant guardianship. The first concerns incapacity due to "mental illness." In this case, the court needs to find that the person:

> is incapable of taking care of himself by reason of mental illness.... The court may require additional medical or psychological testimony as to the mental condition of the person alleged to be mentally ill and may require him to submit to examination. It may also appoint one or more physicians, certified psychiatric nurse clinical specialists, or licensed psychologists, expert in mental illness, to examine such person and report their conclusions to the court. MGL Chap 201(6)(a).

The second justification for guardianship is by reason of "mental retardation." Here, the court needs to find:

> that the person is mentally retarded to the degree that he is incapable of making informed decisions with respect to the conduct of his personal and financial affairs, that failure to appoint a guardian would create an unreasonable risk to his health, welfare and property" MGL Chap 201 Sec 6A(a).

Finally, a guardian may be appointed "for a person who is unable to make or communicate informed decisions due to physical incapacity or illness" MGL Chap 201 Sec. 6(B).

People who are interested in protecting their assets from long-term care might want to structure their affairs so that they never need a guardian, as guardianship can put in serious jeopardy your ability to shelter assets. That is, in order to be able to implement any of the asset protection strategies described in later chapters of this book, the guardian must get permission of the Probate Court. There is a statute by which the guardian can seek court authorization to preserve assets; however, just because the court *can* authorize the guardian to preserve assets does not mean that the court *will* do so. This is one of the fundamental aspects of a guardianship: ultimately, the court is in control of the assets.

In order to avoid guardianship proceedings, your estate plan can include a document known as a "Durable Power of Attorney" (DPOA). If you become incompetent, the holder of your DPOA (called the "Attorney-in-Fact" or agent) can transact your business for you, much as a guardian would do, but *without* reporting to the probate court. If you insert Medicaid Planning provisions in the DPOA, (discussed in later chapters) then the Attorney-in-Fact would be able to act to shelter assets for you. The DPOA can be as simple or as complex as you want. Typical power of attorney provisions allow the agent to:

1. Deposit or invest funds.
2. Collect debts and enforce and settle claims.
3. Buy and sell real and personal property.
4. Endorse checks.
5. Disburse funds for the health, maintenance and support of the principal.
6. Buy, sell and register cars and boats.
7. Employ agents, attorneys, accountants and other professional advisors.

8. Prepare trust agreements.

9. Enter a safe deposit box.

10. Employ strategies to protect assets from long-term care, such as gifting and entering into annuity contracts.

D. Advance Directives: The Health Care Proxy

It is very important for an estate plan to include a Health Care Proxy. Known in some states as an "Advance Directive," this document deals with medical and end-of-life decisions. Essentially, the Health Care Proxy allows your spouse, children or other trusted person you name to make medical decisions for you if you are unable to do so. If you become incompetent and do not have a Health Care Proxy, your family would need to go to Probate Court and seek guardianship, as discussed just above. The law states that the health care proxy only becomes effective if:

> the principal lacks the capacity to make or to communicate health care decisions. Such determination shall be made by the attending physician according to accepted standards of medical judgment. The determination shall be in writing and shall contain the attending physician's opinion regarding the cause and nature of the principal's incapacity as well as its extent and probable duration. This written determination shall be entered into the principal's permanent medical record. MGL Chap 201D Sec. 6.

The health care proxy is not allowed to consent to "suicide or mercy killing," (MGL Sec. 201D Sec. 12). However, "[a]n agent shall have the authority to make any and all health care decisions on the principal's behalf that the principal could make, including decisions about life-sustaining treatment, subject, however, to any express limitations in the health care proxy." MGL Chap. 201D, Sec, 5. The agent is required to make medical decisions in accordance with his understanding of the wishes of the principal.

An interesting issue that has arisen in recent years is the interplay of the Health Care Proxy and the federal medical privacy laws, or "HIPAA." [4] The HIPAA Privacy Rules regulate the use and disbursement of individually identifiable health information and give people the right to determine and restrict access to this information. These rules became effective on April 14, 2003. While a discussion of the rules is beyond the scope of this book, suffice it to say that it is far from clear as to whether those laws permit medical personnel to discuss your case with the person named as health care proxy. (Under the law in Massachusetts, the medical proxy has access to a person's confidential medical records. However, since HIPAA is a federal law, it supercedes any contrary state law.) To eliminate any problem, health care proxy forms should contain a HIPAA authorization which allows medical personnel to freely discuss your condition with the person appointed as your health care proxy. As of yet, Massachusetts law has not been amended to make the Health Care Proxy form "HIPAA compliant." For this reason, it is the practice of the authors to add a HIPAA authorization to the health care proxies that they prepare.

---

4   This abbreviation stands for the "Health Insurance Portability and Accountability Act of 1996."

Unlike many states, Massachusetts does not have a separate "living will" statute. A living will is a document that states that you do not want heroic or extraordinary measures used to actinically sustain life. However, as mentioned above, Massachusetts law gives the person named as your health care proxy the power to make this end-of-life decision, if appropriate. Therefore, it is incumbent on everyone who signs a health care proxy to have this difficult, but crucial discussion with his or her family.

Chapter 3:
The Medicaid Rules

A. The Difference Between Medicare and Medicaid

Medicare is the basic health insurance program available to anyone who is disabled or over 65 and has paid into the Social Security system. Many people believe that Medicare pays for long-term nursing home care. However, people who believe this and who later enter a nursing home are in for a very unpleasant and expensive surprise, since Medicare does **not** cover such care. Rather, Medicare has a very limited nursing home component. If a Medicare beneficiary spends three nights in the hospital and then goes to a nursing home for rehabilitation, Medicare will pay the nursing home in full for the first 20 days, and then in part from day 21 to 100. Medicare supplement insurance will cover the gap. However, once the rehabilitation patient stops making improvement, Medicare and the Medicare supplement stop paying, even if this occurs before expiration of the hundred days. Thus, Medicare for skilled nursing care is meant to be a short-term benefit only. People who need long-term nursing home care are not covered.

B. Three Ways of Paying for Nursing Homes

Since Medicare will not cover long-term care, what will? There are three ways to pay for a nursing home: long-term care insurance, private payment, and Medicaid. [5]

1. Long-Term Care Insurance

Long-term care insurance is a type of health insurance that will pay for prolonged nursing home stays provided that the conditions of the insurance policy are met. Depending on the policy, payment can be for as little as two years, or for as long as a lifetime. The insurance can pay anywhere from a minimal amount of the nursing home charges all the way to payment in full. The better policies come with an "inflation rider," which means that the policy benefit rises each year. Some policies also include payment for home health care.

Since nursing home insurance decreases people's reliance on Medicaid, the government has enacted laws that encourage people to buy this insurance. Under federal law, the premiums for certain long-term care policies are deductible in part as a medical expense. In Massachusetts, holders of certain long-term care policies will be exempt from the Medicaid spend-down and estate recovery rules; *i.e.*, the holder of such a policy will not have to spend down his assets on nursing home care, and the state will not put a claim against those assets once the person dies. In order to qualify for these benefits, the insurance policy must cover

---

5   According to the Federal Centers for Medicare & Medicaid Services, for the years 1980 to 2003, Medicaid paid 46.0% of nursing home costs, private funds paid for 27.9%, Medicare paid for 12.4%, private insurance paid for 7.7% and other sources paid 6.1%. See Centers for Medicare and Medicaid Services, Nat'l. Health Expenditures by Type of Service and Source of Funds, Calendar Years 1980-03, *quoted in* E. O'Brien, "Medicaid's Coverage of Nursing Home Costs: Asset Shelter for the Wealthy or Essential Safety Net," Georgetown University, May 2005, p. 1.

nursing and custodial care in a licensed facility, must pay benefits of at least $125 per day for at least 730 days and may not have an elimination period (*i.e.*, a waiting period for benefits to start) of longer than 365 days.

Unfortunately, there are two significant problems with long-term care. First, it is simply too expensive for many senior citizens to afford, especially in this age of inflationary pressure, rising medical costs and soaring gasoline and home heating prices. Second, not everyone qualifies for long-term care insurance. The insurance companies set standards as to whom they will insure, and, depending on a person's health, he might not meet the company's standards. The applicant must be in good health. For these reasons, one of the criticisms of Massachusetts long-term care insurance exemption mentioned above is that it favors the younger and more affluent – who can qualify for and afford the insurance – and discriminates against the older and less affluent, in short, those who need it most. Under these rules, if you can afford the insurance and can get it, you will be able to protect your assets, and if you can't afford or can't get the insurance, your assets will be at risk. This is blatant discrimination, and is not the way that government should do things. However, it is the new reality.

2. *Private Payment*

Since relatively few people have long-term care insurance, most people who enter the nursing home begin by paying privately. The problem, of course, is that nursing homes are *extremely* expensive. It is not unusual for a nursing home to cost upwards of $8,000 per month, (with some skirting the $9,000 mark) and very few people can withstand such a payment without quickly exhausting their savings. When the money runs out, nursing home residents are forced to turn to the next method of payment, which is Medicaid.

3. *Medicaid*

Medicaid, known in Massachusetts as Mass Health, is a government program that is administered by the states pursuant to federal requirements. It pays for medical treatment and room and board at the nursing home when you have run out of funds. Due to the high cost of the Medicaid program, and also in no small part to the predilection of the current administration and Congress, nursing home Medicaid is under attack. The ways in which the Medicaid rules have been tightened will be explained throughout this chapter and the rest of this book.

a. Applying *for Medicaid*

In order to qualify for Medicaid, you must either live in a nursing home or have a medical need that requires nursing home care. You must also meet certain financial requirements, which will be discussed later. Applications for Medicaid benefits are filed with one of the "Mass Health Enrollment Centers," located in Tewksbury, Taunton, Springfield and Revere. Typically, the application is filed in the Enrollment Center closest to where you live, or closest to the nursing home. A Medicaid application for a senior citizen in a nursing home has four, and sometimes, five parts, as follows:

A. Application form
B. Long-Term Care Supplement

C. Permission to Share Information Form
D. Appointment of Agent/Representative
E. Request for Resource Assessment
   (for married applicants)

After the application is received at the enrollment center, it is assigned to an examiner known as an Intake Worker. The Intake Worker will review the application for completeness. If anything is missing, or if the worker has questions, he or she will send out a questionnaire called an "Information Request." A copy of the Information Request will be sent to the applicant (or his representative) and the nursing home. There is a thirty-day deadline for complying with the Information Request. (If more time is needed, the Intake Worker may grant brief extensions.) If the Information Request is complete, and if all of the Medicaid financial requirements are met, then the application will be approved. If information is missing, however, then the application is denied. The notice of denial will give the applicant another thirty days to file the missing information. If this information is received within this second thirty day period, then the application will be approved; however, the application date will no longer be considered the date that the original application was filed. Rather, the application date will be the date that the missing information was received. This distinction can be vitally important if the applicant is seeking "retroactive benefits." That is, the law allows a Medicaid application to be approved retroactively, up to three months before the application was filed. Let's look at a simple example to explain this concept. Say that Ray falls below $2,000 in assets on January 1. (As will be explained below, $2,000 is the most money you can have to qualify for Medicaid.) For some reason, though, Ray's Medicaid application is not filed until April 1. Assuming that the application is in order, it will be approved, and the state will begin to pay benefits for Ray retroactive to January 1. Now let's change the facts, and say that the application is again filed on April 1, and the Information Request is issued, calling for compliance by May 1. Compliance is made, but it is incomplete. The application will be denied, but Ray will be given an extra thirty days to complete what was missing. Ray complies by filing the missing information on May 15. The application will be approved, but the new application date will be May 15. Retroactive coverage will go back three months, to February 15. Therefore, Ray's delay in compliance will mean that he will be without coverage between January 1 and February 15. There will be a six-week period, from January 1 through February 15, that the nursing home bill will not be paid, making for a very unhappy nursing home administrator.

The above description is really only a brief sketch of the process, which in reality is much more intricate. The key to a successful Medicaid application is in providing the verifications. Verifications are the background documentation that is filed with the application forms and Information Request. At a minimum, the following verifications will be needed:

1. Copy of deed or lease and property tax bill, if applicable.
2. Age and Citizenship – Copy of birth or baptismal certificate, naturalization certificate, or green card.

3. Social Security, Medicare and front and back of private health insurance cards. A copy of the health insurance bill is also required.

4. Proof of marital status, which will be a marriage certificate, death certificate of spouse or divorce certificate.

5. Complete copies of statements, going back at least two years, of all financial accounts, such as bank accounts, investment accounts, stocks & bonds, mutual funds and any other account with a financial value. You will need to explain and document any large or unusual withdrawals, i.e., all deposits and withdrawals of over $1,500. If any accounts have been closed in the past three years (including matured CDs that have been rolled over) you will need a statement showing a zero balance on the closed account and a statement showing where the funds went.

6. Statement of nursing home personal needs account, if any.

7. Life insurance policies and statement of cash value. For term insurance, written proof that there is no cash value will be needed.

8. Copy of durable power of attorney.

9. All trust documents, along with verification of all assets in the trust name.

10. Prepaid burial contract and cemetery deed.

11. Copies of any annuity contracts.

12. Verification of any assets transferred within the 60 months preceding the application. This

requirement applies not only to gifts, but to any asset sold within the relevant time frame. In the case of a house sale, for example, a deed and closing statement will be required, as will proof of deposit of the closing proceeds.

13. Verification of all income, such as Social Security award statements and pension check stubs. If taxes are withheld from pensions, such withholding needs to be stopped.

14. Copy of the past two year's worth of federal tax returns, or a signed authorization allowing the state to obtain these returns from the IRS.

Providing these verifications can be the most tedious and difficult part the application process. However, it is of the utmost importance, as an application will *not* be approved until all verifications have been provided, and all issues raised by the verifications have been explained. The burden of providing the verifications is on the applicant; the Medicaid office will *not* assist you in getting these documents. The Intake Worker will go through every page of the verifications, and will require you to explain anything out of the ordinary. Additionally, deposits or withdrawals of $1,500 or more will need to be explained. Obviously, it is to the applicant's advantage to assemble the verifications and have answers to the expected questions, *before* filing the application. If the applicant waits until the application is filed and the Information Request is issued to provide the verifications, then, in all but the simplest applications, he will be in trouble: thirty days tends to go by very, very fast.

If you are dissatisfied with the results of the application, you can request an appeal that is known as a "fair hearing." The fair hearing is not a "second chance." Rather, it is a proceeding at which you will have to prove that the Intake Worker wrongfully denied the application, whether due to a mistake of fact or a mistake in applying the law. At a Fair Hearing, each side will have the ability to offer evidence and state the legal basis of his or her case. Although the testimony is taken under oath, and witnesses are subject to cross-examination, the proceedings are far less formal than those of a courtroom. The process of claiming a fair hearing is simple and informal; there is a fair hearing application printed on the Medicaid notice of decision. All you do is fill it out, sign it, and mail it within the deadline.

Under Federal law, a nursing home cannot discriminate, discharge or in any way alter the treatment of a Medicaid patient. If, shortly before a private pay patient switches to Medicaid, the facility transfers the patient to a hospital or to another part of the facility, you have cause to investigate, and determine whether the move was medically justified. Additionally, any facility that accepts federal funds, such as Medicare or Medicaid, has no legal right to require that other family members contribute to the payment, or guarantee payment. Any contracts requiring such guarantees are void.

b. *Medicaid's Financial Requirements*
1. General Rules

Medicaid law puts very strict limits on the amount and type of assets that a recipient is allowed to have. Certain types of assets are not counted towards eligibility, and, accordingly, are called "non-countable assets," whereas certain assets are countable. You are allowed to have unlimited non-countable assets (unfortunately, there aren't that many non-countable categories of assets), but there are strict limits on the countable assets you may have. Non countable assets include, among others:

- The home, if located within Massachusetts, and if used as the principal place of residence. Note that only *one* residence is exempt, so that if you have a vacation home, investment property or second home, the non homestead property will be countable. If the spouse (and certain other relatives) are not living in the home, then the state will place a lien on it. Therefore, even though it is not countable, the state will have a claim against the home to the extent of Medicaid benefits paid, so as a practical matter, it might as well be a countable asset. (New federal rules state that home equity of over $750,000 will bar the applicant from receiving benefits.)

- Prepaid funeral contracts, as long as they are irrevocable, *i.e.,* as long as you do not have the right to cancel the contract for a refund. Note that the payment must be for the cost of the funeral. That is, you cannot "overpay," for the funeral, and then get a refund of any unused amounts after the funeral.

- A bank account, not to exceed $1,500, which is earmarked for burial purposes. This account can be in addition to the prepaid funeral.

- One burial plot for the applicant and spouse.

- Property subject to legal proceedings, such as property in probate.

- Income tax refunds.

- One motor vehicle per family

- Cash value of life insurance policies, the face value of which exceeds $1,500.

- Term life insurance, with no cash value.

- Cash assets up to $2,000.

All other assets are countable, with no exceptions. Examples of countable assets are obvious: bank accounts, IRAs and similar retirement accounts, cash value of life insurance above $1,500, stocks, bonds and mutual funds, second homes, second cars, deferred annuities, and *anything* else of whatever kind or description that can be sold or turned into cash. There are special rules for jointly owned assets. As to any jointly owned asset other than bank accounts, Mass Health will presume that all the owners own the asset in equal shares, unless it is proved otherwise. As to bank accounts, the entire amount is deemed available to the Mass Health applicant, unless it is proved otherwise.

As noted above, the home is not countable, though it is subject to the state placing a lien on it. However, due to changes made in 2006 by the Deficit Reduction Act (DRA), there is now a cap on allowable home equity. If the equity in a home exceeds $750,000, then the applicant will not be eligible for Mass Health. An exception is made if the home is occupied by a spouse, child under age 21, or child who is blind or permanently disabled. Starting in 2011, the $750,000 figure will be indexed to inflation. This rule may be waived in the event of "undue hardship." Undue hardship exists when (1) the applicant's health or life would be endangered, or he would be deprived of food, shelter, clothing or the necessities of life, and (2) the medical institution has notified him that discharge proceedings due to non payment of the bill are to be initiated and (3) there is no less costly alternative placement.

If you have countable assets over the allowable limit, you will not be eligible for Medicaid until you have spent down sufficient funds so as to be below the limit. Not surprisingly, this process is known as the "spenddown." Instead of merely spending down, however, you might be able to implement certain very powerful Medicaid Planning devices to preserve most, not all, of your countable assets, and still allow you to qualify for Medicaid.

Medicaid has separate rules for income. In the case of a single person, *all* of the income, except for a "personal needs allowance" of $60 per month plus enough money to pay for health insurance premiums, must be paid to the nursing home. In the case of a married couple, the income of the healthy spouse is not counted, while the income of the institutionalized spouse is counted. The healthy spouse does have the benefit of certain income protections, discussed in more detail below.

2. Division of Assets for Married Couples

Under a law ironically known as the "Spousal Impoverishment" provisions of the Medicare Catastrophic Coverage Act of 1988, the healthy spouse benefits from a certain amount of asset protection. Unfortunately, though these protections are quite meager. In Medicaid parlance, the nursing home spouse is known as the "Institutionalized Spouse," and the spouse living at home is known as the "Community Spouse." Congress, in passing the Spousal Impoverishment law, recognized that it would not be in society's interest to completely impoverish the Community Spouse. Under the Spousal Impoverishment law, the Community Spouse is entitled to keep half of the couple's countable assets, up to a maximum of about $99,500. In other words, the Community Spouse can keep half of the countable assets, or $99,500, *whichever is less.* For example, say Rita and Hal have a house and $300,000 in the bank. Rita goes into the nursing home. Hal can keep the house and $99,500. The "excess" money needs to be spent down. Now let's change the facts. Say Rita and Hal have a house and $100,000. Again, Rita goes into the nursing home. Hal can keep the house and only $50,000, because that amount is less than $99,500. (There is a procedure by which Hal might be able to keep somewhat more, explained later on.) When dividing the assets of a married couple, it makes no difference whose name the assets are in, and it makes no difference who brought the asset to the marriage. Many spouses, especially those involved in second marriages, take false comfort from the fact that they hold their assets in separate names, or in separate revocable trusts, or from the fact that they have entered into a Premarital Agreement. When a spouse involved in a second marriage enters a nursing home, the Community Spouse might be in for an extremely uncomfortable surprise: whose name the asset is in, or whether there is a Premarital Agreement, is *completely irrelevant*. When a couple says, "I do," they are, for Medicaid purposes, consenting to treat their assets as if those assets were jointly held – in the eyes of the law, the marital unit has one pocketbook. The amount of money that the Community Spouse can keep is strictly controlled and limited by federal law, as we have just seen.

Further, the "protection" provided by the Spousal Impoverishment law is not automatic — the Community Spouse must request that it be granted. The procedure to make this request is known as a "Resource Assessment." Once the Institutionalized Spouse enters a hospital or a skilled or intermediate nursing facility and is likely to remain institutionalized for at least 30 consecutive days or more, the Community Spouse is entitled to have the Resource Assessment done. The Resource Assessment does not have to be done at that time, however. It can be done later, as part of the Medicaid application itself, after the spend down has taken place. However, the Community Spouse would be well advised to do the Resource Assessment as early as possible. Since the Resource Assessment is essentially a financial snapshot of the assets on the date the other spouse became institutionalized, it is easier to get the needed financial records shortly after the fact, than months or, sometimes, years later. This is especially true today, when it is quite possible that the bank you have been doing business with for a long time might not exist a year or two from now. The documentation required to process a Resource Assessment is the same as that needed for a full application.

3. Treatment of Income for Married Couples

Once the Medicaid asset tests have been met, the state will consider the income of the married couple. Subject to deductions for the personal needs allowance and medical insurance, the income of the Institutionalized Spouse must be paid to the nursing home in full. However, depending on the couple's circumstances, the Community Spouse may be allowed to keep some of the income of the Institutionalized Spouse, instead of this income being paid to the nursing home. Under federal law, each state must establish a "Minimum Monthly Maintenance Needs Allowance." (MMMNA). The MMMNA must be at least 150% of the federal poverty line for a family of two, and it rises each January 1. The MMMNA currently is $1,650. If the Community Spouse's income is below the MMMNA, he will be entitled to an allowance from the income of the Institutionalized Spouse in an amount equal to raise his income to the MMMNA. If both spouses have a fairly low income, it is possible that, even with a 100% income allowance from the Institutionalized Spouse, the income of the Community Spouse might still be below the MMMNA. In this case, the Community Spouse can request a Fair Hearing for the purpose of allocating him a greater resource allowance. That is, the Community Spouse can be granted a level of assets greater than half the money, or $99,500. There is a sophisticated methodology, dealing with interest rates, of determining how many extra resources the Community Spouse will be allowed to keep. Basically, the Community Spouse will be allowed sufficient assets, which, given a certain interest rate prescribed by law, will bring him enough income so that he will reach the MMMNA.

4. *The Spend down*

Due to Medicaid's strict asset limits, many people need to spend down their assets in order to qualify for benefits. If you need to spend down, there are certain spend down strategies that can help you. As mentioned above, certain assets are not countable for Medicaid purposes. It is perfectly permissible to spend money on non countable assets, as long as you pay fair value for them. For example, a prepaid funeral contract is not a countable asset. If you buy a prepaid funeral, it is paid for out of spend down funds, *i.e.*, the funds that would otherwise have gone to the nursing home, and not the funds protected for the Community Spouse. One car per family is also not countable. Therefore, the Community Spouse can trade in the old car and buy a new one. He or she can also buy furniture and personal items or pay for home improvements and repairs, all without limit, or pay down bills. Care should be taken, however, not to buy items, such as expensive jewelry, artwork, or a luxury car, as such items may be considered to be investments, which would then be countable.

Whether assets are liquidated by making purchases or by paying the nursing home, attention must be given to the tax consequences of the spend down. Many people today hold the bulk of their wealth in retirement assets such as IRAs and 401ks. There are significant income tax consequences when these assets are liquidated. The same is true of appreciated assets such as stocks and real estate, and assets with a taxable and non-taxable component, such as savings bonds and annuities. In planning the spend down, you need to be sensitive to the income tax consequences of liquidating assets. Therefore, it is very often advisable to consult with an accountant or financial advisor prior to finalizing plans as to the order in which assets should be liquidated.

Spending down in accordance with the state requirements, however, can be viewed as a last resort. We have already seen some modest techniques which can minimize what the nursing home resident and spouse have to spend. The field of Medicaid Planning, which we discuss in later chapters, can actually allow you to save the bulk of your wealth – sometimes all of it, while making you eligible for Medicaid.

5. *Estate Recovery*

The process known as "Estate Recovery" is when the Commonwealth attempts to be repaid for Medicaid benefits from the estate of a deceased Medicaid recipient. In Massachusetts, estate recovery is limited to the so-called "Probate Estate," *i.e.*, those assets of a deceased Medicaid recipient which go through probate on death. A few years ago, the state enacted laws which would have made non-probate assets, such as insurance, life estates and joint tenancies, subject to estate recovery. Due to massive citizen complaints, though, these laws were repealed shortly after passage.

Chapter 4:
Medicaid Planning For
Those in a Nursing Home,
or About to Go into One

A. The Ethics of Medicaid Planning

Medicaid Planning is defined as structuring your assets in a way that protects them from being depleted by the nursing home, while making yourself eligible for Medicaid benefits. In the past few years debates have raged in editorial pages and state legislatures across the country about the ethics of Medicaid Planning. The argument against Medicaid Planning is that it artificially makes people eligible for public benefits which were really designed to serve the poor. United States Secretary of Health and Human Services Mike Leavitt, in a February 2005 speech, said:

> Medicaid must not become an inheritance protection plan. Right now, many older Americans take advantage of Medicaid loopholes to become eligible for Medicaid by giving away assets to their children. There is

a whole industry that actually helps people shift costs to the taxpayer. There are ways families can preserve assets without shifting the costs of long-term care to Medicaid. We must close these loopholes and focus Medicaid's resources on helping those who really need it. Doing so will save $4.5 billion during the next decade.

Speech to World Health Care Congress, Marriott Wardman Park Hotel, Washington, D.C., February 1, 2005.

This, and similar arguments, have been made with increasing fervor in view of the federal and state budget crises of recent years. By contrast, here is what the New York Court of Appeals had to say in a 2000 case called *Matter of Shah*:

No agency of the government has any right to complain about the fact that middle class people confronted with desperate circumstances choose voluntarily to inflict poverty upon themselves when it is the government itself which has established the rule that poverty is a prerequisite to the receipt of government assistance in the defraying of the costs of ruinously expensive, but absolutely essential, medical treatment.

We agree with the New York court. In our view, Medicaid Planning is legal, moral and ethical, for the following reasons:

1. Most Medicaid Planning is primarily for the benefit of the spouse, not the children.

As we saw from an earlier chapter, the Medicaid law offers but scant protection for the healthy spouse. The healthy spouse is allowed to keep the home, plus half of the assets up to a cap of approximately $99,500. At first blush, this does not look so bad. A closer look, however, will reveal just how harsh and punitive it is. Remember, the healthy spouse only gets half the assets or $99,500, *whichever is less.* So, for example, if the monetary assets are $120,000, then the healthy spouse can keep only $60,000. If the assets are $100,000, then the healthy spouse can keep $50,000, and so on. This meager amount is all the savings the spouse has to live on *for the rest of his or her life.* With the cost of health care, gasoline, heating fuel, state and local taxes as well as other expenses out of sight, this paltry financial limit on the healthy spouse is a frightening thought indeed.

In our view, it is wrong to have the spouse of a nursing home patient live a life of poverty or near poverty, especially after he or she has worked and saved a whole life to build up a nest egg and avoid living in poverty in old age. It is wrong for this spouse to worry about paying for a roof, furnace, or water heater when those things need to be replaced. It is shameful that the law puts the healthy spouse — more often than not elderly and living on a fixed income — in such a financial predicament of losing their spouse and their assets during the "golden years". In August 1935, President Roosevelt signed the Social Security program into law and said, "We can never insure one hundred percent of the population against one hundred percent of the hazards and vicissitudes of life, but we have tried to frame a law which will give some measure of protection to the average citizen and to his family against the loss of a job and against poverty-ridden old age." It is a shame that the government has not only abandoned this lofty goal, but has embraced the opposite viewpoint. Rather than society protecting, "the average citizen," as FDR said, the government has enacted policies that punish the middle class while benefiting the wealthiest Americans. In our view, Medicaid Planning is not about being an "inheritance protection plan," as Secretary Leavitt said, but is about helping elderly, vulnerable seniors with a spouse in the nursing home end out their years with some degree of financial dignity.

We have also always been of the belief that the number of senior citizens who use Medicaid Planning to shelter their assets is fairly insignificant. An important new study has borne this out. In May 2005, Georgetown University issued a report that said, in part:

Research demonstrates that a large proportion of the disabled elderly in the community (who are at risk of nursing home placement) have limited assets. Many qualify for Medicaid in the community, and most would qualify for Medicaid at admission to a nursing home. Most of the elderly with disabilities in the community have too little wealth to warrant hiring an attorney to arrange an asset transfer. Moreover, studies that look at who pays for nursing home care find that, even though they have limited resources, a large proportion of the elderly pay their own way throughout their nursing home stays, and that the elderly are less likely to rely on Medicaid than would be predicted given their resources.

There is little evidence that large numbers of the elderly are planning their estates for the purpose of gaining easy access to Medicaid in the event they need nursing home care. There is no evidence that they use transfers [of assets] or trusts to significantly shift the cost burdens to Medicaid, and little evidence that those who do transfer sizeable assets gain eligibility for Medicaid.

Georgetown University Long Term Care Financing Project, "Medicaid's Coverage of Nursing Home Costs: Asset Shelter for the Wealthy or Essential Safety Net," by Ellen O'Brien, May 2005, p. 3.

This study confirms what we, as experienced elder law professionals, have known for years, that most people do not use Medicaid planning to shelter their assets, and the study directly contradicts the unsupported statements to the contrary that Secretary Leavitt made in his February 2005 speech.

2. *The Law of Health Care Financing for the Elderly is Irrational and Unfair, and Medicaid Planning is a Response*

The current system of health care financing for the elderly is irrational and unfair. Consider the example of two people, both ages 75. One person develops cancer, and his treatment will cost $300,000. Medicare and Medicare Supplement insurance will cover most of the cost, and financially, he will be in good shape. The other person in our example develops Alzheimer's disease. He will go to the nursing home, and his care will likewise cost $300,000. However, neither Medicare nor Medicare Supplement will pay for his care. So, somewhere along the way society has made the decision that conditions requiring hospital or medical care will be covered, but chronic conditions requiring long-term nursing home care, such as Alzheimer's or Parkinson's, will not. There is absolutely no rational reason for society to cover one medical condition but not the other. Medicaid Planning seeks to correct this imbalance, and give some rationality to a broken system that does not make sense.

3. There is Nothing Wrong With Leaving an Inheritance for the Children

The vast majority of our clients are far from wealthy. They are ordinary citizens who have worked in the trades, in factories or in mom-and-pop type small businesses. By hard work, ingenuity and frugal living, they have paid for a house, educated their children and built up a modest nest egg. For the most part, today's seniors are decent, moral people who have saved, lived modestly, and paid their taxes without complaint over a lifetime. They are the people who have laid the foundation of the success that our society now enjoys.

Most of these people earnestly want to leave a small legacy to their children and grandchildren. Contrary to the opponents of Medicaid Planning, who try to instill guilt over leaving an inheritance, we think that doing so is an honorable thing, and is the right of every citizen. Let us be clear: We are *not* talking of leaving vast fortunes or beachfront mansions to the children at taxpayer expense. That is a different issue entirely. We are talking, rather, about passing down a modest house that someone has spent 30 years paying for, or a relatively small bank account, or a CD that can help a struggling family pay for college tuition. Our clients could very easily have spent the money during their lives, but have chosen not to do so and to live modestly so that they could help their children. No opponent of Medicaid Planning has ever been able to adequately explain why this is a bad thing. We believe that everyone has the right to help and protect their spouse, children and grandchildren, and there is nothing unethical about doing so.

B. Different Types of Medicaid Planning

1. Asset Transfers

In the field of Elder Law, no technique is more misunderstood — or misused — than gifting assets. When used properly, gifting can shelter about half of the assets of someone who is in a nursing home, or about to go into one. When used improperly, gifting can cause Medicaid disqualification, taxes, and loss of assets.

Central to gifting is an understanding of the transfer of asset rules. These rules, stable for over a decade, were revised in February 2006 by the Deficit Reduction Act (DRA). Congress used the DRA to try to substantially cut back on Medicaid planning. Essentially, the transfer of asset rules state that if a gift is made within five years of applying for Medicaid, then the donor (maker) of the gift will be disqualified for Medicaid benefits. The length of the disqualification will increase with the size of the gift. More precisely, the length of the disqualification will be equal to the size of the gift divided by the average private-pay nursing home rate in the state (the "disqualification rate"). The idea is that if you gave away sufficient assets to pay for, say, six months in the nursing home, then you will be unable to qualify for Medicaid benefits for six months. If you give away sufficient assets to pay for one year, you will be disqualified for one year, and so on. Currently in Massachusetts, the disqualification rate is approximately $6,900 per month.

The transfer-of-asset rule ties into another Medicaid concept, that of a "lookback period." Under the DRA, there is a 60-month lookback period for any type of transfer, whether to an individual or to an irrevocable trust. (Formerly, only irrevocable trusts carried the 60-month transfer, and transfers to individuals were subject to a 36-month lookback.) That is, Medicaid can only ask about, or look back on, transfers that have occurred within the past 60 months. If you gave away an asset worth $100,000 to your son 61 months ago, Medicaid will not take the gift into account because the gift fell outside of the lookback period. However, if you gave a $100,000 asset to your son within the 60-month lookback period, then you will be disqualified from Medicaid for a certain length of time.

Under the new rules imposed by the DRA, the Medicaid disqualification does not run from the date of the gift, but from when the person is out of money and would otherwise be Medicaid eligible. Two simple examples will show how this rule works. Say that Uncle Harry gives away $69,000 on January 1, 2006. Under the old rules, he will be eligible for Medicaid ten months later, on November 1, 2006. The new rules, however, work very differently. Let's say that Uncle Harry is perfectly healthy when he makes his gift on January 1, 2006. He suffers a stroke four and one-half years later, and enters the nursing home on June 1, 2010. On that date, he makes the first payment to the nursing home and buys a prepaid funeral contract, and these expenditures reduce his assets to under $2,000. Under the old rules, he would be eligible for Medicaid. Under the new rules, the disqualification as a result of the $69,000 gift made four and one-half years ago first starts to run when Uncle Harry becomes otherwise eligible for Medicaid, *i.e.*, when his assets fall below $2,000, June 1, 2010. The ten-month disqualification will start to run from that time, and will expire on March 31, 2011. Who will pay for the nursing home during the ensuing ten months of disqualification? Uncle Harry can't pay, because he is out of money. Unfortunately, no one knows who will pay. Clearly, Congress did not think this issue through very well when it drafted this law.

Under the DRA, people such as Uncle Harry will be penalized for any gifts they have made during the past five years, regardless of the purpose of the gift. It does not matter that a moderate gift was made exclusively for a purpose other than to qualify for Medicaid. [6] Therefore, the new law, for all practical purposes, prohibits gifting by people who have even a remote chance of needing nursing home care within the next five years and who will have trouble paying for it, *i.e.*, almost all Senior Citizens.

---

6   Actually, one of the Medicaid regulations in Massachusetts states that no transfer of asset penalty will be imposed if the purpose of the gift was "exclusively" for a purpose other than to qualify for Mass Health. However, how would someone go about proving this? Proving someone's subjective intent is extremely hard, and, by definition, cannot be objectively proved. If you make a $50,000 gift to your daughter so she can put a down payment on a house, can you be absolutely sure that, four and one-half years from now, you will be able to convince a Mass Health intake worker that sheltering this money from the nursing home was not lurking somewhere in the back of your mind? Maybe you can, but on the other hand, maybe you can't.

There are a few very limited exceptions to the transfer-of-asset rules that pertain to the family home. The major ones are transfers:

A. To the spouse;

B. To a child who is under age 21 or who is blind or permanently and totally disabled;

C. To a sibling of the applicant if that sibling has a legal interest in the home and was living there for at least a year prior to the applicant's admission to the nursing facility;

D. To an adult child who is living in the house and who provided assistance to the applicant, such that he was able to be kept out of a nursing home for at least two years.

E. To a sibling who has an equity interest in the home, and who resided there for at least one year prior to the individual's admission to the nursing home.

As can be seen, this feature of the DRA, *i.e.*, starting the lookback period after the gift has been made, can be devastating to anyone who has made a gift within the past five years and who does not have enough money to pay for a nursing home. If someone has made a gift for *any purpose whatsoever*, including a gift to charity or church, a wedding gift to a grandchild, a gift of college tuition, or a gift to a child to help him out of a tough financial spot, for example, and if that person goes into a nursing home within the following five years and applies for Medicaid, he could be in some very big trouble: He could find himself disqualified for Medicaid for perhaps a very long time, all for having been good to someone by having made a gift. Except for the very wealthy who can afford nursing homes, we believe that this feature of the law will cause a major reduction in gifting not only in Massachusetts, but possibly in the entire country as well.

Before leaving the topic of gifting, an explanation of the tax consequences of gifting needs to be made. Most people know that you can gift $12,000 to anyone per year without any tax consequences. However, very few people understand the tax consequences of making gifts above this amount. Luckily, in most Medicaid Planning cases, there will be absolutely no gift tax consequences. First, it is important to understand that there is *no income tax* whatsoever on a gift. Rather, the tax burden falls on the person who makes the gift. The donor, or maker, of a gift of above $12,000 to any person in any one year must report the gift to the IRS by April 15 of the following year, on a gift tax return, IRS Form 709. Fortunately, however, each citizen has a lifetime gifting limit, tax free, of $1,000,000. Since the vast majority of people who do nursing home planning have far less than this amount, it is almost always the case that no taxes will be due.

a. *Paying for Five Years and the Reverse Half-a-Loaf*

Two powerful Medicaid Planning devices are derived from the lookback and transfer of asset rules. Both of these devices work for people who are in a nursing home now, or who are about to go into one. First, if you are fortunate enough to be able to pay privately for five years' worth of care, then you can gift all of your assets above that amount and use the remainder to pay for the nursing home. Five years in a nursing home could easily be expected to cost almost $500,000, however, so that very few people will be able to use this option. For those who are fortunate enough to be able to do this, however, it is an option that should be considered. However, it is very important to whom you make the gift. You almost *never* want to gift the asset to your child, because the assets are then subject to your child's liabilities and life circumstances. For example, say your assets are $900,000. You keep $500,000 on hand to cover five years' worth of payments, and gift your daughter the rest. She is married to someone whom you detest. Your daughter takes ill and passes away unexpectedly, and her will leaves all of her money (really your money) to the evil son-in-law. He then remarries, and the money is gone. Or, your daughter gets divorced, and the $400,000 you gifted to her becomes part of her divorce property settlement. Or, your daughter's marriage is fine, but she unexpectedly becomes very ill or has a serious accident, and she needs nursing home care. Although this is unlikely, it can happen. Your money would then go to pay for her care. As you can see, gifting money to your children is fraught with difficulties and uncertainties, and the money just might not be available if you need to get it back.

Therefore, it is *essential* to have the recipient of the gift not hold the funds in his own name, but place them into what is known as a "gift trust," or an irrevocable "creditor protection trust." Such a trust will not die, and will not get divorced, remarried or be sued. It can be structured so as to be protected from creditors. The trust is like a protective wrapper around the money, safeguarding it not only from your children's creditors, but also and whatever trouble they may get into.

Another very powerful technique involving gifting is the so-called "Reverse Half-a-Loaf" strategy. Under the Reverse Half-a-Loaf, it is possible to shelter approximately half of the assets, even if the person is *already in the nursing home, or is about to go into one.* That is, taking into account the amount of assets, income, expenses and the state disqualification rate, it is possible to calculate the amount of money needed to cover the disqualification caused by a lump-sum gift. Factoring in all of these variables, it is generally possible, with a Reverse Half-a-Loaf, to shelter between 40 and 60 percent of the nursing home resident's assets. To take a simple example, say that Helen Smith is a widow, and that she has just entered the nursing home. Her assets consist of $138,000 worth of bank accounts, and she has two children, Emily and Glenn. The first step would be for Emily and Glenn to form a trust. Let's call it "The Smith Family Trust." Helen gifts her $138,000 to the Smith Family Trust, leaving her with under $2,000. Since she has under $2,000, she would be eligible for Medicaid, but for the gift. Recall that under the DRA, the Medicaid disqualification period starts when the person, but for the gift, would otherwise be eligible for Medicaid. The gift of $138,000 would disqualify Helen from Medicaid benefits for 20 months ($138,000 divided by $6,900 = 20). The law also says that for every $6,900 that is returned, one month is shaved off of the disqualification period. Therefore, the Smith Family Trust distributes half of the money, or $69,000 to Emily and Glenn, and they, in turn, give the money back to their mother. The return of the money cuts the disqualification from 20 months to 10. Helen uses the $69,000 that has been returned to her, plus her Social Security and pension income to pay the nursing home for the next 10 months, and, at the end of that time, she will be eligible for Medicaid. The other $69,000 remains in the Smith Family Trust, and is distributed to Emily and Glenn at Helen's death. Half of the money has been saved! Of course, the above was just a simple example which we have used to explain the concept. In real life, the calculation is more complex. Generally, though, the Reverse Half-a-Loaf can shelter about 40% to 60% of the money from long-term care.

Frequently, Reverse Half-a-Loaf planning is done by one of the adult children acting as power of attorney. If this is the case, then *extreme care* must be used in how the Reverse Half-a-Loaf is done. First, the power of attorney must be scrutinized to see if it contains provisions allowing the attorney in fact to make gifts. Assuming that it contains gifting authorization, the attorney in fact must then make a good-faith determination that gifting is in the best interests of the Medicaid applicant. If so, then the proper type of trust must be designed to hold the gifted funds, and the terms of this trust should match, as closely as possible, the terms of the applicant's will.

Brief mention needs to be made of the Health Insurance Portability and Accountability Act of 1996. Section 217 of the Act stated that anyone who disposes of assets with the purpose of obtaining Medicaid assistance is guilty of a crime. Popularly referred to as the "Granny Goes to Jail law," the statute shortly came under heavy criticism from Senior's groups, legal scholars and the bar. The result was that the statute was amended so as to exonerate clients from criminal responsibility, but to impose criminal penalties on paid advisors who counseled clients about the disposal of assets during the penalty period.

Fortunately, attorneys no longer have to worry about the criminal statute. In March 1998, Attorney General Janet Reno, in a letter to then Speaker of the House Newt Gingrich, advised that the Justice Department would not be enforcing the statute, due to serious questions about its constitutionality. At the same time, the New York State Bar Association sued the Justice Department, alleging that the law was unconstitutional. Ultimately, on September 14, 1998, the Federal District Court found that the law was unconstitutional on First Amendment grounds, and entered a permanent injunction against the Justice Department from enforcing it. Therefore, the law, having been declared unconstitutional, and invalidated by the courts, is no longer a cause for concern. While it technically is on the books, no one pays any attention to it any more, and, in effect, it has become a nullity.

2. *Annuities*

Another very powerful type of Medicaid Planning technique involves the use of a certain type of annuity known as an "immediate annuity." With an immediate annuity, you transfer a sum of money to an insurance or annuity company, in exchange for monthly payments of principal and interest back to you. To understand an immediate annuity, think of a promissory note. With a promissory note, you transfer a sum of money to a borrower. In exchange, the borrower pays you back in monthly installments of principal and interest. An immediate annuity is similar. The biggest difference between a promissory note and an immediate annuity, however, concerns the length of the payment term. With a promissory note, the payments can be for any length of time agreed to by lender and borrower. With an immediate annuity, the length of the payment stream is based on the recipient's (*i.e.*, annuitant's) life expectancy. In the case of a married couple, an immediate annuity can shelter money, *sometimes as much as 100%,* from long-term care. This is the result of two different laws pertaining to spenddown in the case of a married couple. Recall from our discussion of the spenddown rules that the Community Spouse is permitted to keep half of the monetary assets, up to a cap of about $99,500. If a married couple has $150,000, the healthy spouse can keep $75,000, and the rest (except for $2,000) would have to be spent down. Significantly, the law says that the spenddown funds do not have to be spent on the nursing home. Those funds can be spent for any purpose, as long as fair value is received and as long as they are spent for the benefit of either spouse. The other relevant law concerns income. The income of the Community Spouse is completely exempt from the nursing home bills of the sick spouse. So, if one spouse is in the nursing home on Medicaid, and the other spouse has a job or otherwise gets income, then such income does not need to be used for the sick spouse's nursing home bill.

The key to annuity planning, then, is to re-structure the finances to convert assets, which are fully countable for the nursing home, to income for the healthy spouse, which is completely exempt. In the above example of a $75,000 spenddown, the healthy spouse uses the spenddown money to buy an immediate annuity. The annuity is structured so that the payments go to the healthy spouse. In this way, the ill spouse immediately qualifies for Medicaid, the monthly annuity payments go to healthy one, and *all* of the spenddown money has been preserved. The risk in this case is that the healthy spouse would him or herself later need to go into a nursing home during the life of the annuity. In this event, the annuity payments will have to be spent on the nursing home.

There are two types of immediate annuities, commercial annuities and private annuities. A commercial annuity is handled through an insurance or annuity company. The advantage of a commercial annuity is that once it is done, there is nothing further to think about. All you need to do is to collect the check every month. The disadvantage of a commercial annuity is in the interest rate. The way the company makes a profit is to invest the money at a higher rate of interest than is paid to you.

The second kind of immediate annuity is known as a private annuity. With a private annuity, an individual, usually one of your children, takes the place of the insurance company. That is, you transfer the money to a child, and he makes the monthly payments to you. The advantage of a private annuity is that the profit that the insurance company would have made with your money is, instead, kept in the family. The disadvantage of a private annuity is that you need to rely on your child or children to make the payments each month.

The DRA made significant changes to the annuity rules. Under the DRA, the annuity needs to state that it is irrevocable and non-assignable. There can be no right to cash in, or surrender, the annuity. In the case of a married couple, the Community Spouse may be named as the primary beneficiary of the annuity, but the Commonwealth of Massachusetts must be named as secondary beneficiary to the extent of Medicaid benefits paid. In the case of an unmarried person, the Commonwealth must be the primary beneficiary to the extent of Medicaid benefits paid. If the annuitant lives to collect all of the payments, however, then the annuity has been completed, and the Commonwealth has no beneficiary rights.

Deferred Annuities

One more word about annuities is in order. Generally, there are two types of annuities. One is the immediate annuity described above. If done correctly, as we have just seen, an immediate annuity can help to shelter money from the nursing home. The other type of annuity is a deferred annuity. Many Senior Citizens use deferred annuities for investment purposes. In a deferred annuity, you deposit the money with the insurance company. Much like a bank CD, the insurance company pays interest on the principal of the annuity, and it grows in value. One major difference between a bank CD and an insurance company deferred annuity, however, is that a deferred annuity can be "annuitized," *i.e.*, surrendered to the insurance company, and converted to an immediate annuity of the type described above. Some unscrupulous insurance agents or investment advisors sell deferred annuities to Senior Citizens, with the false explanation that the annuity is "protected" from the nursing home, or that all the nursing home can get is the interest, and not the principal. Such statements are outright deceptions.

A deferred annuity is a completely countable asset, offering no nursing home protection at all. The ability to quickly annuitize a deferred annuity, or convert it into an immediate annuity, is actually of little practical value, since virtually any monetary investment can be quickly sold and converted to an immediate annuity. Therefore, all seniors should be cautioned about the use of deferred annuities as Medicaid planning tools, since they have no use at all for this purpose.

3. *Life Care Contracts*

There is another type of Medicaid Planning technique known as a Life Care Contract. Let's take a look at Janet. Four years ago her father died and for the past three years she has been caring for her aging mother. Her mother has about $80,000 in the bank, and, if Janet were to put her mother into a nursing home, that money would only last about 10 months. Perhaps given Janet's high degree of involvement with her mother's care, a Life Care Contract should be considered. This is a formal agreement where Janet becomes Mom's care manager. Even though Mom is in the nursing home, if done properly, Mom can pay Janet for her care management services. For example, if Janet spends approximately 1½ hours per day caring for Mom, that's nine hours per week (*i.e.*, six days per week times 1.5 hours per visit). Mom can agree to pay Janet $10 per hour or $90 per week for her services.

In and of itself, that wouldn't be very exciting. Mom can agree to have Janet act as her care manager for as long as Mom lives. In other words, Mom can pay Janet $4,320 per year (*i.e.*, $360 per month times 12 months) and Mom can make this payment in a lump sum for Mom's life expectancy. So if Mom has a life expectancy of 11 years, she can pay Janet $47,520 (*i.e.*, $4,320 per year times 11 years) and she can pay the $47,520 *up front,* in one lump sum.

This will allow Janet to provide Mom the care she needs and still allow Mom to qualify for Medicaid. Please understand that this is the "short version" and that this type of planning must be handled in a very specific manner. But, when done properly, it can be used to solve Janet's dilemma.

4. *Life Estate Deeds*

One method of sheltering the house would involve placing it into another's name, presumably an adult child or children, reserving a life estate to the grantor. A life estate is the right to live in property owned by another for life. For example, you transfer your house to your son, so that ownership is in his name. However, the deed to your son says that you have the right to live in the property until your death. A life estate deed, like any other gift or transfer, is subject to a five-year lookback period. If you have a life estate in property and then release (or waive) the life estate, your release will also be subject to a five-year lookback.

One advantage of a life estate deed is that the house is protected from the children's creditors, since the parents' right to live in the house is paramount to any attachment or execution that a creditor may make against the property. Additionally, the life estate means that the child still receives the benefit of the stepped-up tax basis at death. The chief disadvantage of a life estate deed is that the parent loses control of the property, since the parent is unable to sell the property without the consent of the child or children who own the property. Additionally, assuming that the children do consent, then distribution of the purchase price can get complex. The parent is entitled a certain percentage of the purchase price that is equal to his life estate, and the children are entitled to the remainder. (The IRS has tables that specify the relevant percentages.) There will also likely be tax consequences to the children, both from accepting the money and then from giving their portion back to the parents.

If you have a life estate in property and receive Medicaid benefits, the Commonwealth will place a lien against the value of your life estate. If the property is sold during your lifetime, the Commonwealth then will be able to get repaid for the Medicaid benefits out of your share of the life estate. If the property is not sold during your life, however, the lien will be dissolved at your death, and the Commonwealth will not have the right to be repaid from the house proceeds.

Due to the potential problems with life estate deeds, the authors generally do not recommend them as Medicaid planning techniques. In the correct circumstances, though, and if the parties understand and are willing to take the risks associated with such deeds, then they can be useful.

5. *Deed with Mortgage Given Back*

Sometimes it suits the client's purposes to give a deed outright to the children without retaining a life estate. For example, say that the parents live in the house, but are themselves unable to pay the rising expenses, such as taxes and heat. One of the children is willing to assume payment of these expenses, on the understanding that the parents will deed the house to him or her. Or, the parents might simply want to give the house to one of the children outright. The problem here is the new lookback rules of the DRA. If one or both of the parents needs nursing home care within five years of making the gift, the new lookback and transfer of asset rules may make them completely ineligible for Medicaid. How can we meet the parents' goal of making the gift, while protecting them if either of them needs nursing home care within the next five years?

The answer is a gift deed with mortgage given back. That is, the parents and child enter into a written agreement that says that the parents will deed the house to the child. If the parents need nursing home care within the five years after the gift has been made, the parents will pay for it out of their own assets and income. If the parents' assets and income are not sufficient to cover five years' worth of payments, however, the child to whom the house was gifted will then make up the difference, out of his or her own funds, until the lookback period has expired. In order to give the parents security, the child gives the parent a mortgage on the property. The mortgage guarantees the child's obligation to fulfill the agreement. If the child breaches the agreement, whether willingly or not, the parents can foreclose on the mortgage, and get the property back. In this event, the Medicaid disqualification period is eliminated, and the parents will be able to use the home equity to pay for the nursing home. If the parents do not need nursing home care within the five years, then the mortgage is discharged, and the child will own the property free and clear. This use of a mortgage to secure the obligations of the child provides the parents with complete protection, since, the parents are assured that they can get the property back if he needs it. Once the lookback is over and the parents no longer need the security of being able to get the property back, then the mortgage obligation ends also.

Chapter 5:
Trusts and Medicaid Planning

Trusts are essential tools in Medicaid Planning, and the DRA has made at least one type of trust even more important than ever. In this chapter, we will look at three different types of trusts that can be used to protect assets, the Irrevocable Medicaid Trust, the Pourover Trust and the Revocable Trust with Medicaid Triggers. All of these trusts are for people who have time to plan, *i.e.*, people who are healthy now and want to protect themselves and their families should they become ill and need nursing home care in the future.

A. *The Irrevocable Medicaid Trust*

For years, the Irrevocable Medicaid Trust has been the workhorse of Medicaid Planning. With this trust, you receive all of the income and control the investments of the trust. Through the trust, you can buy and sell assets, including real estate such as the family home. On your death, the trust passes to the heirs without probate. During your lifetime, however, the trust is irrevocable and is subject to a five-year lookback period. The lookback concept is the same as that described earlier, when we spoke about gifting. In other words, the trust assets are not protected from long-term care until five years have elapsed since the assets were put into the trust name.

The disadvantage of the Medicaid Trust is that you do not have direct access to the principal. The rule is simple – if you can get the money, the nursing home can get the money. If you can't get it, the nursing home can't get it, either. To have access to principal in the trust, you work with the children. Say you set up a Medicaid Trust. You are the trustee, and you name your children as beneficiaries. Now say that you want to obtain principal from the trust. (Remember, you are entitled to the income, in any event.) You, as trustee, take the money you want, and distribute it as a gift to one or more of your children. As stated earlier, you can gift them $12,000 each per year without any tax reporting. Your children then take the money and gift it back to you, and you use it as you wish. Everyone uses the Medicaid Trust differently. Some people use it to protect their house only, while others use it to protect some of their liquid assets, such as stocks or CDs.

The Medicaid Trust is ideal to protect your house (or other real estate) from long-term care. Since a house is not liquid, like money, the children have no involvement at all. You are free to sell the house through the trust if you want to, and buy another one in the trust, and the new one will be protected, as well. This trust is a "grantor trust" for federal tax purposes. Therefore, you are still entitled to the capital gains tax exclusion if you sell the house, you can still deduct mortgage interest and property taxes, and your heirs still receive the benefit of the stepped-up tax basis at your death.

The DRA has made the Medicaid trust more important than ever. Under the DRA, you are completely disqualified from Medicaid if you have over $750,000 worth of equity in your house. If, however, the house is part of the Medicaid trust, then, for Medicaid purposes, it is not in your name. Therefore, assuming that the lookback is over, you don't have to worry about the DRA's equity limit. Even if the house is worth over $750,000, you will not be barred from obtaining Medicaid.

B. *The Pourover Trust*

The Medicaid Trust has long proven supreme as an asset protection tool. Yet, there is another type of trust that approaches asset protection in a completely different way, the Pourover Trust. The Pourover Trust is revolutionary, in that it allows a married couple to shelter assets from the nursing home using a trust that is completely revocable, that can be amended at any time while both spouses are living, that has no waiting period, and that allows the married couple to have unfettered access to their money.

The Pourover Trust makes clever use of what is known as a "testamentary trust" coupled with a will and revocable trust. In order to understand the Pourover Trust, you need to understand the concept of a "testamentary trust. A testamentary trust is a trust within a will. Let's say that Lorenzo signs a will leaving his assets to his wife Barbara. Lorenzo dies, and Barbara goes into the nursing home. The assets Barbara inherited from Lorenzo belong to her, and, as such, are subject to being spent on the nursing home. To avoid this result and protect the money, Lorenzo writes his will in a different way. Instead of leaving the money outright to Barbara, his will says that he is leaving the money to her in trust for her maintenance, support, lifestyle, comfort and care. The trustees are the children of Lorenzo and Barbara. Thus, at Lorenzo's death, instead of Barbara inheriting the money directly, the money is held in trust for her care. This type of trust (a trust within a will) is known as a testamentary trust. The federal law which underlies Medicaid states that if a testamentary trust is written in the correct way, and the beneficiary of that trust enters a nursing home and applies for Medicaid, the principal of the testamentary trust will not be available to the nursing home; *i.e.*, it will be sheltered. Therefore, the money in Lorenzo's trust does not have to be spent for Barbara's nursing home care.

In all but the most unusual case, one spouse will die before the other. Since we do not know who will be the first to die, we create a joint husband and wife revocable trust. The assets to be protected from the nursing home are placed into the name of that trust. While both spouses are alive, they can use the trust assets as they wish, without any restrictions or involvement of the children. They can even revoke the trust if they want to. The trust states that on the first death, some or all of the assets are to "pour over" to the estate (*i.e.*, the will) of the spouse who has died. The will creates a testamentary trust for the benefit of the surviving spouse. That testamentary trust says that the funds are to be used for the care, comfort and maintenance of the surviving spouse, to maintain the spouse in his or her accustomed standard of living. Usually, one or more of the children act as trustees. Since testamentary trusts are exempt from the nursing home, the assets in the trust are protected. The nursing home does not have access to those assets.

On of the beauties of the Pourover Trust is that there is no waiting or lookback period. It is effective immediately on the first death. The trust can also be tailored to fit the needs of the client. That is, there is no requirement that all of the assets be placed into the trust. Whatever the couple wants to protect from the nursing home is put in the Pourover Trust, and the rest of the assets can be left out. It is our prediction that the Pourover Trust will become used more and more often as a Medicaid Planning Tool.

C. The Revocable Trust with Medicaid Triggers

For those people whose primary objective is probate avoidance, and who are only secondarily interested in protection of assets from the nursing home, the "Revocable Trust with Medicaid Triggers" may be appropriate. The Revocable Trust with Medicaid Triggers allows your family to implement Medicaid Planning for you in the future, if, due to illness or incapacity, you are no longer able to do implement on your own. As we saw in an earlier chapter, a Revocable Trust is a legal document that serves the same purpose as a will, but which avoids probate at death. However, the Revocable Trust goes beyond mere probate avoidance, in that it also has provisions for a successor trustee, usually one of the children, to manage the trust in the event you become incompetent.

"Medicaid Triggers," simply stated, are those things that your trustee or attorney-in-fact can do for you to protect assets. The more important of these things have been discussed in earlier chapters. Medicaid Triggers are detailed provisions that specifically allow your trustee to do the following things, among others:

A. Represent you before the state Medicaid authorities, both in applying for benefits and in claiming a fair hearing;

B. Apply for a Resource Assessment;

    C. Secure the Minimum Monthly Maintenance Needs Allowance;

    D. Convert countable assets into non-countable ones;

    E. Employ the caretaker child exception;

    F. Do a Reverse Half-a-Loaf;

    G. Enter into a commercial or private annuity;

    H. Enter into a Life Care Contract;

    I. Use whatever other techniques Congress may create or allow in the future.

When you create a Revocable Trust with Medicaid Triggers, it is also essential that you insert the Triggers into the Durable Power of Attorney that is usually done with the Trust. The reason is that there are certain assets, such as IRAs, 401(k) s and other tax-deferred retirement accounts that cannot be put into the name of the trust. Additionally, you may have forgotten to put all of your other assets into the trust name. Therefore, the successor trustee of the Trust does not have the ability to do any Medicaid Planning with these assets, since they are not a part of the Trust. If, however, the Durable Power of Attorney contains the Triggers, then the Attorney-in-Fact would be able to shelter these assets, as well. Every person who sets up a Revocable Trust should consider adding Medicaid Triggers, since the triggers "set the stage," so to speak, for your Successor Trustee to engage in Medicaid Planning should the need arise later on.

D. *The Irrevocable Life Insurance Trust*

This is a special trust for people who need estate liquidity or a tool to create cash to offset Federal or State Estate Taxes.

An Irrevocable Life Insurance Trust (ILIT) is a type of trust specifically designed to own life insurance on you the retiree. The retiree makes gifts of cash to the trust which in turn purchases life insurance on the estate owner. This creates a form of leverage where premiums can purchase significant tax free life insurance benefits if the trust is established correctly. The trust is the owner and beneficiary of the life insurance and the value of the insurance is not part of your countable estate. Placing proceeds within the trust can create several benefits for your family; it keeps the proceeds out of the taxable estate, it protects the insurance proceeds from creditors, it protects your beneficiaries and avails a very cost effect method to settle an estate. Reviewing the feasibility of the Irrevocable Insurance Trust may save your family unnecessary taxes upon your death. We will cover the Massachusetts and Federal Estate tax issue in more detail in the next chapter which will illustrate the taxing problem many seniors unknowingly are facing in the Commonwealth.

Chapter 6:
Federal and
Massachusetts Estate Taxes

When someone dies, his or her estate may be subject to a tax known as the estate tax. There are two levels of estate taxation, state and federal. Many people confuse estate taxes and inheritance taxes, but they are quite different. Inheritance taxes are levied on the beneficiary when he or she inherits assets. Estate taxes, by contrast, are levied not on the beneficiary, but rather on the assets which a decedent owns at death. In other words, the tax is assessed and paid even before the beneficiary receives the inheritance. Generally, all of the assets that a decedent either owned or had a legal interest in at the time of death are subject to estate taxes, as are gifts over a certain amount that the decedent made during life. If the total of the assets owned at death and gifts are above a certain threshold, then the estate tax is imposed, and if the assets are below that threshold, there is no tax. The executor has a choice of valuing the assets either at the date of death or at a so-called "alternate valuation date" that is six months after death.

Certain deductions against the tax are allowed, including debts of the decedent, expenses of administering the estate such as legal and accounting fees, charitable bequests, and assets passing either to the surviving spouse or to certain types of trusts for the benefit of the surviving spouse. If a tax is due, it must be paid within nine months from the date of death. A 2001 law known as the Economic Growth and Tax Relief Reconciliation Act states that the federal estate tax threshold will be $2 million for the years 2006 through 2008. The threshold will rise to $2.5 million in 2009. In 2010 there will be no federal estate tax at all, but then in 2011 it will come back at a $1 million threshold.

In addition to the federal estate tax, individual states may have their own estate taxes. Before January 1, 2003, the estate taxes of many states, including Massachusetts, were tied to the federal estate tax. Under the laws in effect at that time, a percentage of the federal estate tax owed to the IRS would instead be paid to that state. The IRS, in turn, allowed estate taxes paid to the state to be a dollar-for-dollar credit against the federal tax. In this way, even though the state and federal estate tax loads were calculated separately, the tax paid to the state would be subtracted from the tax paid to the IRS. The states, in effect, were said to "sponge off" the federal tax, and hence these state estate taxes were known as "sponge taxes."

The Economic Growth and Tax Relief Reconciliation Act referred to above not only raised the thresholds that were subject to tax, but also phased out the availability of states to take advantage of, or "sponge off" of, the federal tax. Thus, the amount of money that states could raise from their own estate (sponge) taxes was lowered. That is, the increased exemption thresholds meant that fewer estates were subject to tax to begin with, and the sponge taxes imposed by those states were eliminated. To counter the expected decrease in revenue, some states, including Massachusetts, responded by "decoupling" their estate taxes from the federal estate tax. Decoupling means that the state estate tax would be calculated without reference to the federal estate tax. As of 2006, Illinois, Kansas, Maine, Maryland, Massachusetts, Minnesota, New Jersey, New York, North Carolina, Oregon, Rhode Island, Vermont, Virginia, Wisconsin and District of Columbia have decoupled their estate taxes from the federal tax. In Massachusetts, decoupling became effective for the estates of people dying on or after January 1, 2003.

Under the Massachusetts version of decoupling, the filing thresholds and exemption amounts are lower for the Massachusetts estate tax than for the federal estate tax. The Massachusetts filing threshold is $1 million. Therefore, at least until 2011, when the federal threshold also becomes $1 million, the filing requirements and exempt amounts must be determined separately for Massachusetts and federal estate tax purposes. Since the Massachusetts thresholds are lower than the federal thresholds, many more estates will be subject to the Massachusetts tax than the federal tax. Due to the rapid escalation of real estate values in recent years, many people who do not think of themselves as wealthy will nevertheless be subject to the Massachusetts estate tax.

Prior to decoupling, when the Massachusetts tax was tied to the federal tax, a typical "dual revocable trust" estate plan would include an individual trust for each spouse. The trusts were each funded with approximately half of the total estate. After the death of the first spouse, his or her trust assets were allocated into two separate sub-trusts, the so-called "A-B Trust." The first sub-trust, funded with the amount exempt under federal law, is known as the Family Trust. Under the Family Trust, assets are available to the surviving spouse and children (but principally the surviving spouse) pursuant to an ascertainable standard, usually health, maintenance, education and support. In this way, the trust assets can be used for the support of the surviving spouse, but are held in a way that those assets are not part of his or her taxable estate. The rest of the assets belonging to the trust of the first spouse to die pass into another sub-trust called the "Marital Trust." The Marital Trust provides the surviving spouse with all of the income. It also often gives the trustee discretion to distribute principal as necessary for the surviving spouse's maintenance and health. Unlike the Family Trust, the Marital Trust is a part of the surviving spouse's taxable estate. In other words, when the second spouse dies, the Marital Trust assets are included among the assets that are subject to estate taxes. However, the Marital Trust is not taxed at the death of the first spouse, since it is subject to the 100% Marital Deduction. Upon the surviving spouse's death, the assets left in the Family Trust and Marital Trust pass to the heirs. There are two different ways that the Family Trust and Marital Trust are funded. One way is called "formula funding." With formula funding, the executor is required, pursuant to a predetermined formula, to allocate the assets among both trusts. The formula typically states that the trusts are funded in such a way as to make sure that there is no tax at the first death. The second method is known as "disclaimer funding." With disclaimer funding, the decision as to how to fund the trusts is made by the surviving spouse. He or she "disclaims," or refuses to receive, assets of his choice. These disclaimed assets pass to the Family Trust. The assets not disclaimed go to the Marital Trust, or can go directly to the spouse.

Under the A-B type of estate plan, there are no estate taxes at the first death, and, at the second death, estate taxes are either eliminated or minimized. A simple example will show how this plan works. Say that Henry and Lois have an estate of $2.2 million, and say that Henry dies in 2011, when the federal estate tax exemption will be $1 million. They each have a simple will that leaves all of the assets to the surviving spouse. When Henry dies in 2011, his will leaves all of his assets to Lois. An estate tax return will be filed, since Henry's estate is over the $1 million threshold. No tax will be due, though, since the money being left to Lois is subject to the Marital Deduction; i.e., it is deducted from the estate tax. Some years later Lois dies, having an estate of $2.2 million. Since the estate tax exemption is only $1 million, a tax will be due on $1.2 million dollars.

To avoid this result and minimize estate taxes, Henry and Lois enter into dual revocable trusts. Each trust is funded with half the estate, or $1.1 million. Henry dies in 2011. The federal estate tax exempt amount, or $1 million, goes to the Family Trust. The excess of $100,000 goes to the Marital Trust. The $100,000 that goes to the Marital Trust is subject to the 100% Marital Deduction, and the $1 million that goes to the Family Trust is not taxed either, as it is equal to the exempt amount. Lois has use of Henry's funds, as she is the beneficiary of both trusts. At Lois' death, she has $1.1 million in her name. The first million dollars is not taxed, but the $100,000 in her name is taxed, as is the $100,000 in the Marital Trust that Henry left. Thus, the amount subject to tax at the second death is only $200,000, instead of $1.2 million.

Prior to decoupling in 2003, estate planning for a married couple with a taxable estate was not difficult, as the "A-B" trust referred to above minimized, if not eliminated, all taxes. Now that the Massachusetts and Federal thresholds are different, though, the landscape has completely changed. If the Family Trust is funded with an amount of money that is less than the Federal exemption ($2 million) but more than the state exemption ($1 million) an estate tax will be due at the first death. For example, if $2 million were to go into the Family Trust, there would be a Massachusetts estate tax due on $1 million, and this tax would be $99,600.

Fortunately, the Massachusetts Department of Revenue (DOR) has addressed this issue. In a directive known as Technical Information Release 02-18," DOR has ruled that an executor may elect (i.e., claim) a marital deduction for Marital Trust property for Massachusetts' estate tax purposes without requiring the executor to make the same election for federal estate tax purposes. [7] In other words, the Marital Trust for Massachusetts tax purposes can be different for the Martial Trust for federal estate tax purposes. Therefore, the amount going into the Family Trust is limited to the amount exempt for both state and federal purposes,

---

[7]   Technically, this election is called a "QTIP Election." The term QTIP stands for Qualified Terminable Interest Property, which is derived from Section 2056(b)(7) of the Internal Revenue Code. Typically, and executor makes a QTIP election equal to the amount of the taxable estate over the federal exclusion amount. By definition, the federal exclusion amount is not subject to tax, and the property subject to the QTIP election is subject to the 100% marital deduction. Therefore, a proper QTIP election can eliminate estate tax at the first death.

i.e., $ 1 million. The difference between the Massachusetts exemption and the federal exemption goes to a special Massachusetts Marital Trust. The remainder of the estate goes to the Marital Trust allowed under federal law, or is distributed outright to the surviving spouse.

As a result of these changes, many Massachusetts estate plans need to be re-written, or, at the least re-evaluated. Essentially, instead of splitting the trust of the first to die into two trusts (the A and the B), the trust of the first to die might have to be split into *three* trusts, or three shares. First, there will be the Family Trust. Second, there will be the Massachusetts QTIP Marital Trust, and third will be a Federal Martial QTIP trust or a simple bequest to the surviving spouse. Any married couple with an estate over $1 million (or approaching $1 million) should be concerned about this issue and needs to have their estate plan reviewed.

Chapter 7:
The Social Security Tax Trap

In 1993, a modification to Social Security benefit taxation caused one of the largest tax increases to affect seniors in the history of our country. Very few seniors understood the significance of this change, and even fewer are taking advantage of planning techniques to reduce or eliminate this increase.

Before 1993, seniors paid taxes on half of their Social Security benefits if their combined income was $25,000 for individuals or $32,000 for married couples. In 1993, the portion of taxable Social Security increased to 85 percent, and individuals with "provisional" incomes above $34,000 and married couples with "provisional" incomes above $44,000 were subject to the higher rate of taxation. Those with provisional incomes below $25,000 and married couples with provisional incomes below $32,000 pay no taxes on their Social Security benefits.

Simply explained, provisional income is the sum of a person's wages if still employed, interest on his money, dividends from his investments, the net of capital gains/ losses, any pension income (exclusive of Social Security), and any annuity or IRA distributions.

To this total, add one-half of the person's annual Social Security benefit, and if the sum of these is greater than $34,000 for a single taxpayer or $44,000 for a married couple, you fail the provisional income test, and your Social Security benefit is now taxed at the 85% threshold.

This increase has caused many seniors to pay much more in taxes over the last decade. Many have done nothing to counter the increase; they just pay more federal income tax.

Avoid the Mistake. Review your most recent tax return. Specifically, review line 8a (interest). For many seniors this number is large because of the large stockpiles of cash in savings accounts, certificates of deposit, or treasuries. The interest this money produces in the bank or in government bonds may be causing you to "fail" the provisional income test. The interest being generated on these accounts may be the cause of the 85% Social Security threshold!

Consider a shift to tax-efficient or tax-deferred investments to reduce line 8a or 9b on the tax return to a level where you would "pass" the provisional income test and enjoy the Social Security benefit without counting it as a taxable event. This is what you expected when you entered the system in the first place.

There are several techniques to properly eliminate or reduce the implications of this tax problem.

Using a tax-deferred annuity to solve the problem is but one method. In addition to an annuity, shifting assets to "tax- efficient" planning also works well to reduce the exposure to the added tax.

Here is an example of a client couple that is currently "failing" the provisional income test:

Mr. and Mrs. John Client have been enjoying their retirement years. Their total household income is $55,000, and they have an adjusted gross income of $52,000. Not all Social Security benefits are taxable, as shown below.

Wages	$ 0
Interest (line 8a)	$ 20,000
Pension	$ 15,000
Social Security (line 20a)	$ 20,000

Determining how much of Social Security is taxable is a two-part process as described earlier.

First, determine the household income exclusive of Social Security benefits paid.

Interest (line 8a)	$ 20,000
Pension	$ 15,000
Household income	$ 35,000

Second, add the household income and one-half the annual Social Security benefit.

Household income	$ 35,000
One-half annual	
Social Security benefit	$ 10,000
	$ 45,000

$45,000 is greater than the top of the provisional income threshold of $44,000. As a result, this couple is taxed on 85 percent of their $20,000 Social Security benefit, increasing their taxable earnings by $6,850

How to Return Social Security Back to Tax-free *Status.*

Mr. and Mrs. Client decide to shift most of their bank cash (which they don't plan to use but like to keep safe) into a fixed annuity. The interest is not taxable unless withdrawn. The results:

Wages	$ 0
Interest (line 8a)	$ 3,000 (1)
Pension	$ 15,000
Social Security	$ 20,000

First, determine the household income exclusive of Social Security benefits paid. Next, add one-half of the annual Social Security benefit.

Household income	$ 18,000
One-half Social Security benefit	$ 10,000
	$ 28,000

This $28,000 is less than the bottom provisional income test of $32,000. As a result, the clients are taxed on *none* of their Social Security benefit. This decreases their taxable earnings by nearly $7,000 accomplished simply by shifting the manner in which they allocate their savings.

Many seniors make the mistake to focus on estate taxes and forget about using techniques that prevent the confiscation of wealth via the income tax. The income tax consequences of your actions or inactions can make a world of difference for you and your family. Spend some time reviewing your tax returns, and consider seeking advice to determine what planning opportunities would be best suited for your goals and objectives.

D.   Client maintains over $50,000 in bank for emergencies or opportunities

Chapter 8:
Net Unrealized Appreciation

Many retirees have accumulated very large 401(k) balances or other qualified plans as a result of a career's worth of savings. For some, a large percentage of your plan consists of highly appreciated individual company stock. The tax savings you can generate using the NUA (net unrealized appreciation) technique can make a significant impact on your financial and estate planning.

Unfortunately, many retirees and many advisors make a fundamental mistake: they roll the qualified plan rich in employer stock to an IRA. Often retirees and advisors assume rolling to an IRA is the only option available. On the surface this seems like the standard operating procedure, but if this option is exercised you may cost your family thousands of dollars in additional taxes they should not have to pay!

A. *NUA Explained*

NUA occurs when an employer-sponsored plan allows the employee to purchase employer securities as part of the qualified retirement plan. The Internal Revenue Service treats these securities held inside the plan differently than it treats other assets such as cash and mutual funds when an employee retires. When the employee rolls over his qualified plan to an IRA, he has the opportunity to withdraw his employer securities and pay income tax on the cost basis (not the current value) and capital gains tax on the gain if he sells the employer securities. The cash, mutual funds, or other investment accounts will roll over to the IRA and are not taxed until withdrawn. (See IRS publication 575.)

Case Study

Mr. Smith, age 65, has a 401(k) plan valued at $500,000. $250,000 is mutual funds and $250,000 is company stock. The basis on the company stock is $50,000. Assume Mr. Smith is in the 25% federal income tax bracket.

Option 1: Normal rollover approach

Mr. Smith rolls the entire account to an IRA. Any normal distributions he takes will be taxed in the 25% federal income tax bracket. At age 70½, he will be forced to take required minimum distributions (RMD) and pay taxes on these distributions in his then applicable (assumed 25%) tax bracket. (See IRS Publication 590.)

Option 2: NUA rollover approach

Mr. Smith rolls the stock out of the 401(k) plan. The basis on the stock is $50,000, and he must pay ordinary income tax on the basis of $12,500 ($50,000 x 25% tax rate). The stock is transferred to a non-qualified account. No additional taxes are owed on the stock until Mr. Smith sells it. Assume he does sell the stock. He pays capital gain tax on the sale vs. ordinary income and is thus taxed at 15% (current maximum capital gain tax rate), not 25%. This creates an immediate tax savings of 10%. Shares sold under this technique are taxed at long-term capital gain tax rates (up to the NUA) regardless of the length of time between the roll-out and the sale of the stock and short- or long-term gains on any additional gain beyond the NUA based on the time of sale. If he does not sell the stock, there are no additional taxes beyond the ordinary income tax due on the rollout. All other remaining funds are rolled to an IRA.

B. *Benefits of NUA*

First, by utilizing the NUA approach you will reduce your overall tax burden on the 401(k) plan and have the opportunity to use capital gain tax rates vs. ordinary income tax on $200,000 of the value of the account.

Second, by reducing the amount rolling into the IRA you will reduce the required distribution amounts when you reach age 70½. Required minimum distributions are calculated on the year end balance of the IRA, and if you remove the value of the stock from the account it will not be included in the RMD calculation.

Third, capital gain tax rates are significantly lower than the current income tax rates.

These tax savings can be used to fund long-term care and other estate preservation strategies using funds that otherwise would have been lost to taxes!

C. *Drawbacks*

This technique is designed primarily for those above age 59½. The early distribution penalties apply to those who elect this option under age 59½, and a 10% early distribution penalty will apply. The technique, however, may still be a viable option under these circumstances, as the penalty tax only pertains to the "basis" of the roll-out and not the full value of the stock.

NUA does not enjoy a "stepped-up basis" at death. When reviewing your overall estate planning objectives you must be aware that, unlike other highly appreciated securities you may own, the NUA stock will not receive the increase to market value at death and may present a large capital gain tax to the beneficiary. A plan to liquidate out of the NUA stock may be necessary to prevent erosion due to the tax the beneficiary will pay.

Chapter 9:
The "Stretch" IRA

The single largest asset for many retirees other than their primary residence is their Individual Retirement Account ("IRA"), and most are completely unaware of the tax nightmare that awaits the beneficiaries of these accounts if the account holders have not properly established a plan to pass this tax-deferred asset to their spouses and children.

In 2001, the Internal Revenue Service overhauled the rules pertaining to mandatory distributions from IRA accounts, and as a result some excellent planning opportunities are now available. Today, with proper planning, your IRA accounts can live on for your family long after you are gone.

After an IRA owner's death, a spouse can roll the IRA into his/her name. This "spousal" rollover approach is widely known as a preferred planning technique to protect the spouse. Where most IRA planning goes awry is when the spouse dies and the children plan to inherit the asset. If the surviving spouse names a "designated" beneficiary of the IRA account, the beneficiary can withdraw the funds from the IRA over his or her life expectancy after the parent dies. The planning potential of this technique is tremendous. Under the old rules, the beneficiary would simply cash out the parent's

IRA account and pay the income taxes on the distribution, resulting in massive taxes for most beneficiaries. With the new rules, the beneficiaries have a planning opportunity to take simply the RMD (Required Minimum Distribution) based on their life expectancy, and the remaining account balance can continue to grow on a tax-deferred basis. This technique is known as the "Stretch IRA." The beneficiary can elect to remove more than the required distribution at any time if he needs additional funds.

Case Study

Mr. John Smith, age 65, has an IRA valued at $100,000. Let's assume that he earns 6% on this IRA and will be taking only his Required Minimum Distributions once he is age 70½. Assume he has one child whom he names beneficiary of his IRA. His child (Bill) is age 40. Mr. Smith's required distribution schedule will look like this:

Now let's assume Mr. Smith lives until age 85. When he dies, his son is age 61. His son has two choices

First, he can simply cash out Dad's IRA (no stretch) and pay the income taxes due.

Lump Sum Account Liquidation in 2026
Total distributions	$157,758
Federal income tax on total distribution	$ 41,230
Net after-tax to Bill	$116,528

Over 26% lost to taxes.

Second, Bill stretches the IRA.
Required Distributions from 2026 through 2050
Total distributions $367,647
Federal income taxes $ 60,735
Net after-tax income $306,912

Only 16.5% lost to taxes.

With no stretch planning Bill will inherit $116,528, but with the stretch IRA planning he will inherit $306,912. With proper planning the IRA account will become a family heirloom and a multigenerational asset transferring event. (*The above calculation assumes son is married filing joint return and has taxable income of $50,000 excluding the required distributions.*)

How the Stretch Technique Works
Bill must begin taking required distributions from his father's IRA based on his own life expectancy starting the year following his father's death. His father's IRA is now worth $160,758, and his son, now age 61, must take a minimum distribution of $6,465.

Mr. John Smith's IRA
Assuming 6% Return on Investment and Taking Only RMDs

	Age	Required Distribution	Account Value 12/31
2005	65	0	106000
2006	66	0	112360
2007	67	0	119102
2008	68	0	126248

2009	69	0	133823
2010	70	4884	136968
2011	71	5169	140017
2012	72	5469	142949
2013	73	5787	145738
2014	74	6123	148359
2015	75	6479	150782
2016	76	6854	152976
2017	77	7216	154938
2018	78	7632	156602
2019	79	8031	157967
2020	80	8447	158998
2021	81	8883	159655
2022	82	9337	159898
2023	83	9810	159682
2024	84	10302	158961
2025	85	10741	157758

Bill must be listed as a "designated" beneficiary on the IRA beneficiary election form for the stretch option to be valid. The easiest way to understand a "designated beneficiary" is a beneficiary with a birth date. When the son notifies the custodian of the death of his father, he will most likely need to furnish a certified death certificate and also establish a beneficiary IRA account with the custodian. At that time the IRA provider will move the assets from the decedent's IRA into the "inherited" IRA account. Keep in mind the account will stay in the name of the deceased for the beneficiary's benefit but does not roll over into the son's IRA accounts.

Potential Pitfalls

If Mr. Smith failed to name a beneficiary or he named his estate as the beneficiary, his son would have only up to 5 years from the date of death to remove the value from the IRA account. This does not leave much planning opportunity.

If Mr. Smith names a trust as beneficiary, there are numerous potential negative consequences for his son. In most cases it is best to name the beneficiaries of the IRA accounts by name. The son will either use the 5-year rule to remove the IRA assets or, best case, he may be able to use the remaining life expectancy of Mr. Smith. Obviously Mr. Smith's life expectancy would be much shorter than his son's.

The current custodian who holds the IRA may not honor the stretch technique. This is a common but little understood problem with the IRA account. You should review the custodial agreement signed when you established your IRA account to see if the provider will allow the stretch. Surprisingly, not all custodians allow this to occur. The income tax ramifications of not stretching are severe. If your custodian does not honor the stretch you may want to consider moving your IRA account to a provider who does.

The power of the stretch IRA provides you with the opportunity to focus on multigenerational planning while maintaining 100% control of the account during your life.

Chapter 10:
IRA Tax Planning and the Power of the ROTH IRA

The largest transfer of wealth in the history of our country has begun. Many retirees have accumulated very large 401(k) balances or other qualified plans. For many the company retirement plan is the single largest asset other than their primary residence. Many retirees have planned properly for the disposition of their real estate but have neglected planning for the retirement account.

"The Jobs and Growth Tax Relief Reconciliation Act of 2003" has created wonderful planning opportunities for the informed senior. The tax code was enacted back in 1913, and with the tax package of 2003 we are enjoying the "luxury" of some of the lowest tax brackets in our country's history.

Current tax brackets (2006):

<u>10%</u>   Married couples earning less than $15,100 and single people earning less than $7,550 in taxable earnings are taxed in the 10% tax bracket.

<u>15%</u>   Married couples who earn less than $61,300 and single people who earn less than $30,650 in taxable earnings are taxed in the 15% tax bracket.

25%   Married couples who earn less than $123,700 and single people who earn less than $74,200 in taxable earnings are taxed in the 25% bracket.

Food for thought: Our government is allocating a huge amount of resources to fight the war on terrorism and the war in Iraq. Medicare is in a state of crisis. The Pension Benefit Guarantee Corporation (PBGC) is having solvency issues, and our nation's deficit and debt are reaching epic proportions while at the same time we are enjoying some of the lowest tax brackets since the tax code was adopted! Sooner or later our nation will have to change either its spending or our tax structure.

Retirees have been trained to avoid taking distributions from their IRA portfolios for two primary reasons. First, many are comfortably living on their Social Security benefits and pension incomes. Second, when retirees take money out of the retirement account they must do something they have been trained to avoid... pay income tax on the distribution. Many seniors delay the distribution event until it becomes mandatory at age 70½. (See IRS publication 590.)

This is often a major financial planning mistake! One of the largest planning mistakes retirees make when it comes to the IRA account is waiting too long to begin the distribution process. Here's why. The IRA account is tax-deferred, *not* tax-free. When one spouse dies, the survivor is now forced to file a tax return as a "single taxpayer." Review the brackets for single people versus married couples. Married couples enjoy much wider 10% and 15% tax brackets versus single people. In fact, the brackets are cut in half! Many widows and widowers suddenly find themselves jumping into higher brackets and pay more income taxes when they become single taxpayers. Unfortunately, this is not a rare occurrence; it happens all too often. Finally, upon the survivor's death, the IRA is often taxed to the heirs at even higher tax brackets!

With some foresight, you can make the outcome much different.

First, review your tax return. Many seniors actually enjoy the 0% tax bracket, and most married couples are within the 10% or 15% tax bracket. The technique described next works best within these tax brackets. Taxes are eventually due on the IRA. The question is: should you prepay the tax now at the low brackets or delay?

Step 1: If you are already over 70½, take the MRD as required by law out of your IRA. If under age 70½, proceed directly to step 2.

Step 2: Using your previous year's tax return as a guide, run the math to determine what sources of income were reported and what the taxable income was. This is to be a guide. Please remember to consider any additional withdrawals you have taken from your IRA accounts, capital gains from the sale of any investments you hold, pension increases, and/or wages if you worked any part of the year.

Step 3: With this information, forecast what the taxable income will be for the current year.

Step 4: If you are "enjoying the luxury" of the 0%, 10% or 15% bracket, consider "converting" IRA assets to the Roth IRA to the extent that the you will remain within these low brackets. Caveat: you must review your Social Security benefits for inclusion into this calculation.

When you properly utilize this technique you will create *a tax-free* legacy. There will be no required distributions or additional taxes for the surviving spouse. When one spouse dies, a jump in brackets is less likely because there is no required distribution to pass through the single person's bracket. Even if there is not sufficient time to convert the entire IRA to the Roth, you have still reduced the IRA account value for the MRD calculation, resulting in a positive impact on your overall tax planning.

The Roth IRA provides a "one-two" punch by allowing you to reduce the pitfalls in the tax code for single taxpayers while creating a *tax-free* legacy for the family.

Chapter 11:
A Call to Action

If the readers of this book are like most of our clients, they are senior citizens who have worked a lifetime building up a nest egg. They have worked hard, paid their mortgage, paid their taxes, provided for their families and have put money in the bank. Rather than complain or give up when life put obstacles in their path, they have kept on doing what they were taught as children: be diligent in their work and make the best of it.

This generation has been the most successful in history in saving and investing money, and, as this book has shown, there are two forces that can strip them of what they have saved over a lifetime and make it much harder to pass anything to their children and grandchildren: the nursing home and the tax system. Dying in our country and specifically in Massachusetts can present a myriad of taxing obstacles to avoid. Becoming disabled in the Commonwealth and needing long-term care services can rapidly wipe out a lifetime of savings.

As we have demonstrated in this book, our government has instituted policies towards senior citizens that we believe are on the wrong track. Rather than honoring and protecting seniors, our laws allow confiscation of wealth.

The government is steadily taking away strategies and techniques that seniors and their families can use to protect themselves. Yet, as this book has shown, there are still powerful methods of asset protection that remain. Yet it is also clear that time is running out. If you have made it to the end of the book, then you have shown that you are interested in protecting your wealth for you and your family, and not for the nursing home operator or the government. The choice is yours to make. You can protect your family if you enact the techniques available to you.